J. Pritchett 151433

D1443106

Fourscore

By VANCE HAVNER

Fourscore

Living Beyond the Promise

Vance Havner

Introduction by William B. Sigmon, Jr.

Fleming H. Revell Company
Old Tappan, New Jersey

Scripture quotations in this volume are from the King James Version of the Bible.

Permission to quote from the following songs is gratefully acknowledged:

" The Family of God" by William J. and Gloria Gaither. © Copyright 1970 by William J. Gaither. International copyright secured. All rights reserved. Used by permission of The Benson Company, Inc., Nashville.

"Sweeter As The Years Go By" by Lelia N. Morris. © Copyright 1912. Renewed 1940 by Nazarene Publishing House. Used by permission.

" The Love of God" by Frederick M. Lehman. © Copyright 1917. Renewed 1945 by Nazarene Publishing House. Used by permission.

Library of Congress Cataloging in Publication Data

Havner, Vance, 1901–
    Fourscore: living beyond the promise.

    1. Meditations. I. Title.
BV4832.2.H3348   242   82-3823
ISBN 0-8007-1307-9   AACR2

Copyright © 1982 by Vance Havner
Published by Fleming H. Revell Company
All rights reserved
Printed in the United States of America

LIFE Pacific College
Alumni Library
1100 West Covina Blvd.
San Dimas, CA 91773

It is my wish and pleasure to dedicate *Fourscore* to the growing number of students who are being helped by the Havner Fund. Their letters to me and their evidences of genuine Christian experience, along with their progress in preparation for Christian service, bear witness to God's blessing upon the work of the Fund.

Vance Havner

L.I.F.E. BIBLE COLLEGE EAST
LIBRARY
CHRISTIANSBURG, VA

052506

UBRARY
Alumni Library
1100 West Covina Blvd
San Dimas CA 91773

CONTENTS

Introduction

A group of Christian businessmen in Greensboro, North Carolina, will always remember October 16, 1981 as a most special day, for it marked the eightieth birthday of their fellow citizen of Greensboro, Vance Havner. As one who has had the joy of knowing Dr. Havner for many years, I was glad to be among those who, months before that "most special day," quietly laid plans for a surprise birthday banquet in Greensboro. We looked on the occasion as a unique opportunity to honor not only a good friend but a faithful servant of God who has ministered the Word of God for more than sixty-seven years.

Dr. Havner was obviously very moved when the hour arrived and he was ushered into the filled banquet hall in Greensboro. More than four hundred of his friends, many of them from out of state, applauded him. Others who were unable to attend sent their greetings—among them Billy Graham, T. W. Wilson, Jerry Falwell, Dr. Paul Freed, George Sweeting, Jack Wyrtzen and Dr. W. A. Criswell.

To Dr. Havner's great surprise, George Beverly Shea was among those present and sang several of Dr. Havner's favorite hymns. The Reverend Roy C. Putnam, pastor of the Trinity Church of Greensboro, presided over the banquet in an eloquent manner and introduced those who made special presentations in honor of Dr. Havner. They were:

Albert S. Lineberry, Sr., representing Dr. Havner's home church, First Baptist Church of Greensboro; Dr. C. Mark Corts, pastor of Calvary Baptist Church of Winston-Salem and

past-president of the Baptist General Convention of North
Carolina, representing the Baptists of the state; William R.
Barbour, Jr., chairman of Fleming H. Revell Company, pub-
lisher of 31 books by Dr. Havner, presenting the Revell
Achievement Award for 1981 to Dr. Havner; Ronald Muffley,
representing the Bible Broadcasting Network which airs Dr.
Havner's messages on four radio stations; Dr. J. Allen Blair,
president of Glad Tidings, Inc., presenting to Dr. Havner a
Book of Remembrances containing letters of greeting from
people throughout the United States.

J. Robertson McQuilkin, president of Columbia Bible College, read an original poem, "Getting Home Before Dark," explaining that he had composed it after hearing Dr. Havner
preach a sermon by the same title. McQuilkin also made the
final presentation of the evening, unveiling a portrait of Dr.
Havner which was painted by his talented wife, Muriel
McQuilkin.

Dr. Havner wore a broad smile for the entire evening, but to
those of us who looked on, that smile seemed even broader
when two college students took their turns in addressing the
audience. They were Kevin Wilson and Michael Stewart, se-
niors at Columbia Bible College, both of whom were being as-
sisted in their education by the Vance H. Havner Scholarship
Fund. Christian businessmen established the Fund in Febru-
ary 1978 to help young people who are training for full-time
Christian service. The audience was told that since its beginning, more than 135 scholarships have been granted to deserv-
ing students, many of whom would have been unable to con-
tinue their education without financial aid. The testimonies of
Kevin Wilson and Michael Stewart were special gifts to Vance
Havner on his birthday.

Grady Wilson, evangelist with the Billy Graham Evangelis-
tic Association and a friend of Dr. Havner's for over forty
years, delivered the main address of the evening. He punc-
tuated his heartwarming message with many of Vance

Havner's famous sayings in "the Havner dialect," bringing obvious delight to our honored guest.

Following the message, Dr. Havner went to the podium and paid special tribute to the Christian men and women—especially his parents—who encouraged him when he began his ministry. And he challenged his listeners to serve the Lord faithfully "to the end of the race." His closing request was that we pray with him that he would "get home before dark."

David H. Petty, another close friend of the author-preacher for many years, brought the benediction, giving thanks to our Lord for the faithful ministry of His servant and for the memorable evening together. All of us who took part were greatly pleased because it brought honor to our Lord and much joy to God's faithful servant, Vance Havner, whom we had the privilege of honoring.

William B. Sigmon, Jr.
President
Vance H. Havner Scholarship Fund
P.O. Box 1048
Greensboro, North Carolina 27402

Preface

The ninetieth Psalm tells us that the days of our years are "threescore and ten" and, if they be extended to eighty, yet their span is but trouble and sorrow. To which most octogenarians would say a loud "Amen"! But eighty is an enviable mark and all the more so if we can reach it foursquare as well as fourscore! The dictionary says foursquare can mean "unyielding, firm."

Eighty can find us stubborn and churlish on one hand or on the other pleasantly agreeable to anything with a grandfatherly tolerance of the status quo. Either position is a mistake. To be firm in principle and sweet in spirit is a rare attainment whether eighty or otherwise.

Solomon lived a full life and is considered to be the wisest man of all, but no man ever made a bigger fool of himself. His career premiered in wisdom, peaked in wealth and perished with women. Birthdays can mean anything. What is important is not how long you have been on the road but how far you have traveled.

As the old King James puts it, Paul had a desire to finish his course with joy. He advised young Timothy to give attention to Doctrine, Dynamic and Discipline—"Take heed unto the doctrine . . . stir up the gift of God" and "endure hardness, as a good soldier of Jesus Christ." The man who can balance those three by the grace of God is a success at any age.

Such a man will not be faultless but he can be blameless. Like Paul he can have a conscience void of offence toward God

13

and men. He can be vertically right with God and horizontally right with men.

One of the top prize winners in the Bible was Caleb. He was already eighty-five when he faced his greatest challenge and opportunity. He might have settled for a comfortable retirement, but instead of asking for a molehill he said, "Give me this mountain." He tackled the giants and succeeded because he claimed the promise and counted on the presence of God. There is no ground here for the comfortable retirement of preachers as long as they can preach. God does not call us to preach until we are sixty-five; He calls us to preach—period!

There is nothing special even about fourscore, but if we reach that mark God grant that we shall be foursquare! And may our prayer be, "Now also when I am old and greyheaded, O God, forsake me not; until I have shewed thy strength unto this generation, and thy power to every one that is to come" (Psalms 71:18).

Vance Havner

Fourscore

1

The Unseen Hand

"We cannot always trace God's hand but we can always trust God's heart." Spurgeon said it and it is true indeed. But as the years lengthen we can see in retrospect what once showed no rhyme nor reason and we can begin to trace His hand as well as trust His heart. What did not add up then on my little computer now falls into place in the diagram of His purpose. We see through a glass as in a riddle but as time goes on the riddles fade and reality begins to show through.

I can see now His hand in why I grew up on that Carolina hilltop, a happy little boy tramping the woods with his shepherd dog, fed on the Bible, *Pilgrim's Progress, Foxe's Book of Martyrs.* I can see now also why my godly father bought twenty volumes of literature, from the *Odyssey* to *Alice in Wonderland,* and why I pored over these classics although much of what I read was over my head. The words rubbed off on me and I began to build a vocabulary while I started writing little things about Bible characters, doting on history, Napoleon and Theodore Roosevelt, bird watching and browsing over the *Literary Digest,* the *Time* magazine of those days.

It makes sense to me now that I came along in the early 1900s of young America, "the Good Years," before 1912 was crepe-bordered by the sinking of the *Titanic* and everything was brought to an awful halt by World War I in 1914. That span of years after the Spanish-American War from San Juan to Sarajevo was a blessed interlude that will never return.

I can trace the Unseen Hand in my countrified bringing up in those horse-and-buggy, cotton-picking, possum-hunting,

17

corn-shucking times with country church revivals back in the days before the family left the fire-side, let out by auto while the world came in by radio. A country boy can learn city ways, but a city boy cannot learn country ways. You have to grow up there. The original, old-fashioned hillbilly was homegrown. He cannot be produced any other way.

I can see God's hand in my coming to Jesus as a little boy. I saw no visions and dreamed no dreams, and years later I was uneasy when I heard the lurid testimonies of converted tough characters, uneasy lest maybe I had not been converted at all. Today when converts from awful lives of sin tell their story—and thank God for every one of them—the congregation "oohs" and "ahs" but let a man tell simply of being kept from childhood by the grace of God and the reaction often is "so what?" A story of being healed of cancer is top news but to tell of good health to old age by the same God who heals the sick is poor show biz!

I can discern the Lord's hand in the fact that I never knew the time when I did not feel that I should be a preacher. I do not explain that but I always felt that the Lord "done laid His hand on me." We have come to a day of cold American professionalism in all fields and the mystery, the majesty, the mystical have disappeared generally from the ministry. But in those days preachers did not just "decide" to preach as lawyers make up their minds to practice law and doctors opt for medicine. Young Samuels may not hear the Lord's actual voice today but they are called of God by many inward impressions, the Scriptures, leadings, circumstances, counsel. Some thought my father made a preacher out of me. He was happy when he saw the course of my life, but I was not a prophet by profession, nor the son of a prophet by parentage but a prophet by Providence. "The Lord took me" was Amos' only credentials and that is enough for any prophet today.

The Unseen Hand was behind my Boy Preacher years. I began at twelve and went about preaching in town and country churches. This was not worked up by human planning; word just got around, I was invited and crowds came out of curiosity. Many went to Bethany to see Lazarus after he was raised from the dead but they also saw Jesus. Curiosity is not the best motivation for going to church but some come for that reason and see Jesus before they leave. Curiosity put Zaccheus up a tree and Jesus brought him down!

A very irregular and incomplete schooling may seem not to have been the Lord's leading. I remember how the principal of the first Christian school I attended advised me to blaze my own trail. I did not follow the prescribed course, never went to seminary, and such a record disqualifies a would-be preacher in most eyes today. But some of the pulpit giants came from that category. I am not one of the giants and if I were a father I probably would have told my son to go the usual route of preacher training if he had chosen to be a minister. I did not travel the beaten path and the years since have shown me that in my case it was the best course for the kind of work God called me to do.

God does not always send His prophets through the conventional assembly line lest they come out wearing a stamp that does not become them. Fig pinching seems poor preparation for Amos, and Amaziah may view him with scorn. Micaiah was the odd number after four hundred false prophets bade Ahab and Jehoshaphat go up against Ramoth-gilead and prosper. This world hates the four-hundred-and-first prophet, as Joseph Parker said long ago. God's hand often passes up the wise, mighty and noble for a Moody or a Billy Sunday and a Billy Graham without benefit of theological training. I find myself mischievously wondering how Amos would have addressed the Rotary Club in Bethel or how John the Baptist would behave before a Monday Minister's meeting!

During the Twenties there came a deviation which might appear to be a break in divine guidance, but I can see now the Hand that overruled. After the World War, I was enamored to some degree with the liberalism of which Harry Emerson Fosdick was the outstanding champion. I thought the Gospel

should be adapted more to the modern mind which turned out
to be not so modern and not much mind. I preached that way
for a while but eventually gave up my pastorate and went back
to my old home in the hills. All doors were closed to my ministry. I read J. Gresham Machen's *Christianity and Liberalism*
which helped me and I came back to the old faith. I had to go
back to my first pastorate for three years and preach it straight.
I can see now that God overruled and the experience taught
me how to detect the beginnings of such thinking in young
preachers. Having been along that road I might be able to say a
warning word in season.

Ten years as a pastor filled up to good purpose one decade of
my early ministry. Five of those years were spent in a country
church where I walked everywhere. I did not own an automo-
bile until I was sixty-six. I stayed in a home in an upstairs room
warmed by a wood-burning stove, studied by a kerosene lamp
and drank water from a bucket. There was time to meditate, to
be still, to live at an unhurried pace. Sometimes I paddled a
boat down Newbegin Creek to a favored spot where I wrote
my first book, *By The Still Waters.* It is still selling although
other books of mine are out of print.

The Unseen Hand is most evident as I look back now on my
second pastorate, five years in the First Baptist Church of
Charleston, South Carolina, the oldest Baptist church in the
South, begun in 1683. I love old Charleston and can never
repay the debt I owe to those peaceful walks down around the
waterfront, the hours of study in my room in the old St. John
Hotel. It was a time when I was much exercised about a deeper
Christian experience and found much help in an old book,
Deeper Experiences of Famous Christians, given to me by
Grandma Russell, a dear old saint. John 7:37–39 became a
precious passage. Today when church life runs all the way
from rigor mortis to St. Vitus, I am thankful that God's hand
led me to our Lord's prescription: thirsting, coming, drinking,
believing, overflowing. Nowadays Satan has scored a point in

making us so afraid of extremism about the Holy Spirit—which abounds indeed—that we may miss the true in our fear of the false. We can be so wary of getting out on a limb that we never go up the tree!

While I was still in Charleston, writing for Christian periodicals and doing my early books, doors began to open in all directions for preaching. I am a Southern Baptist and most of my preaching is in Baptist churches, but inter-denominational Bible conferences opened other fields. A preacher should belong to a local fellowship but be ready to minister wherever God leads. I can see from experience this double ministry in my own denomination and also to churches at large. The Unseen Hand has created opportunities no booking agent could ever have arranged!

But along with open doors come adversaries. Opportunity brings opposition. Do not imagine that total dedication to God means easy going thereafter. Take a firm stand for God and you become a target of the devil. Casual Christians know nothing of the spiritual warfare we read about in Ephesians. How could they? The average church member doesn't even give the devil enough trouble to get his attention! For two years I was beset by nervous exhaustion, insomnia and depression. How could I undertake a full-time traveling ministry? How could I sleep in a different bed every week when I couldn't sleep much in my own bed every week!

But deciding to make the venture, I resigned from my church and set out. On my first trip I became ill and was forced to cancel my first engagement and go to Florida where I had declined an earlier invitation. There I met Sara Allred and we fell in love. Frail as I was, I had little to offer, but she was willing to start a new life with a half-sick preacher who had little money and was not at all sure he could do the work he had undertaken. Sometime ago I found letters I had written to her (sent with three-cent stamps!) trying to persuade her to go with me. I felt that God was in it and yet in trying to convince her I was also trying to stabilize myself. As I read these letters now, I am convinced as never before that the Unseen Hand was at work when the circumstances said "Impossible."

Sara and I were married in 1940 and for 33 years we traveled over the country with a blessed ministry and ever-opening doors. "Can I doubt His tender mercy who through life has been my Guide?" The piece I found most difficult to fit into the mosaic of God's will for my life came along in 1973. At the beginning of that year I had been much exercised about my own spiritual life and found myself saying, "Lord, at any cost bring me to the point where I can truthfully sing,

> Once earthly joy I craved,
> Sought peace and rest;
> Now Thee alone I seek;
> Give what is best.

In 1973 Sara went to be with the Lord. In my *Daily Light* I had read what my Lord said about Lazarus, "This sickness is not unto death, but for the glory of God, that the Son of God might be glorified thereby." I claimed that verse and believed that Sara would be healed. But when she died I remembered that Lazarus died too. Then I felt that God would be glorified in her passing and He was. I wrote *Though I Walk Through The Valley,* and the response to that little book has been greater than to all my other books. God has been glorified and I see now by faith His Unseen Hand was in control so that while we do not understand how, we know that all things do work together for good to God's children.

These years since Sara went away have been the loneliest in my life. Longing for the touch of a vanished hand and the sound of a voice that is still becomes acute some days and "chronic" most of the time. At the same time these have been the most blessed times ever. Never have so many dear people pressed my hand and said, "You've been a blessing to me." God has opened more doors than I could ever enter. Yet I remember that Dr. Jowett said, "We are not always doing the

most business for God when we are busiest." It may all end
soon but while

> I may be in heaven tomorrow
> I'll love Him and serve Him today.

I thank God for the Unseen Hand, sometimes urging me
onward, sometimes holding me back; sometimes with a caress
of approval, sometimes with a stroke of reproof; sometimes
correcting, sometimes comforting. My times are in His hand. I
am graven on the palms of His hands. No one can pluck me
out of His hand. I call that "having the situation well in hand!"
To some this may seem a hand-to-mouth life, but it is—from
His hand to my mouth!

An old popular song said, "I'm forever blowing bubbles."
Most of us are doing just that and the bubbles are always
bursting. Instead of spending my days blowing bubbles I have
sought to use them by being a blessing. I trust Him as "Lord of
the years that are left to me." I long to finish my course with
joy and "get home before dark." There is nothing morbid
about being homesick for heaven. Paul longed to depart and be
with Christ which is *far* better.

The Unseen Hand may be obscured at times by the fogs of
circumstance but just because we cannot see the sun on a
cloudy day doesn't mean that it isn't there. I close as I began,
"We can trust God's heart when we cannot trace His hand."
Soon the puzzle ("we see through a glass as in a riddle") will
clear up and we shall know as we are known.

2

A Summary of Faith

Today as I walked in the woods there congealed in my mind a summary of my faith which might be helpful to someone else although others probably can write one that is far better. It is good to position ourselves as to where we stand, what we believe and what we seek to be and do as Christians. Of course, no statement is ever completely adequate. No matter what verbal receptacles we use, something always spills over and cannot be said satisfactorily.

I began: "Trusting Christ as my Saviour, confessing Him as my Lord and receiving Him as my Life." Of course, all Christians begin with Christ as Saviour, fewer confess Him as Lord and almost none get around to knowing Him as their Life. I do not mean that we are to partition our experience into categories. We may take Jesus for all He is and spend the rest of our days learning more and more about who and what He is. But "Life" includes a field not usually covered in "Saviour" and "Lord." Of course He is also many other things—Bread and Light and Shepherd and Door and Resurrection and much more; but "Saviour," "Lord" and "Life" sum it up best.

I continued: "I would live by the daily conscious appropriation of the Living Christ by faith for body, mind and spirit." This means the Living Christ for the Total Man, my every need. But this must be "according to God's Word, God's Will, my need and my faith"—the four "accordings." To illustrate: this means physical healing if such is in line with these four "accordings." God did not heal Paul of his thorn in the flesh although Paul was used to heal others. We must distinguish between occasional healings and Christ as life for the body quickening us physically as much as is necessary for our glorifying Him. We shall find in Christ enough of everything we need for body, mind and spirit to do what He wants us to do as long as He wants us to do it.

So I add the purpose of this appropriation of the Living Christ, "that His resurrection power might be released in me to the extent that God is glorified and His purpose carried out in conforming me to the image of His Son." That is the "purpose" so often overlooked in Romans 8:28 and we cannot claim the promise of all things working together for good unless we are the called according to that purpose.

And, lastly, "that I may know Him and HIS, the power of His resurrection, the fellowship of His sufferings and conformity to His death" and "that I may make Him known."

Putting it all together we have: "Trusting Christ as my Saviour, confessing Him as my Lord and receiving Him as my Life, I would live by the daily conscious appropriation of the Living Christ for body, mind and spirit, according to God's Word, God's will, my need and my faith, that His resurrection life might be released in me to the extent that God is glorified and His purpose carried out in conforming me to the image of His Son; that I might know Him and HIS, the power of His resurrection, the fellowship of His sufferings and conformity to His death; and that I might make Him known."

This sums up to me what I mean by saying, "To me to live is Christ."

3

My Fourfold Prayer

I breathe a fourfold prayer these days. It covers just about every conceivable turn my life could take. I begin with "Even so, come, Lord Jesus." I will settle anytime for His return! It may be any time, morning or midnight, and I remember the little motto I saw somewhere that might well hang before us every moment—PERHAPS TODAY! This allows for no date-setting, no undue excitement, waiting on a mountain top somewhere clad in white. Just a calm happy assurance that any day could be the Great Day on the calendar of God.

My second prayer is the outward expression of an inner longing "to depart and be with Christ which is far better." "Homesick for heaven" is no morbid emotion of pilgrims bored with earth's dissatisfactions. It is a perfectly normal and healthy longing of God's child, exile and alien as he is in this world, who would gladly come running if His Master beckoned him to come home. In this earthly tabernacle we groan, earnestly desiring to be clothed in our new Easter outfit. How sweet to wake up some morning and find we are home! God grants to some of His own what dear Pappy Reveal of Evansville Rescue Mission used to mean when he said, "I want a quick get-away." God heard him and granted a sudden takeoff for heaven, with no long slow death, no pining away in a home for the old folks. It can't be for all of us but there's no harm in wishing and whispering it to our Father once in a while.

But if that is not to be, a third petition is in order. Paul mentioned that alternative when he wrote, "Nevertheless to abide in the flesh is more needful for you." I would pray for *an ex-*

tension of time such as God granted Hezekiah, *an enlargement of coast* such as He granted Jabez, and *an enduement of power* such as He gave Elisha—strength from above to do my stint here below, to finish acceptably the charge I have from God.

One possibility remains. The Lord may not return in our lifetime. It may not please Him to take us quickly, gently, or let us just go to bed on earth and wake up in heaven. It may fall our lot to go in some tragic accident, or after years of suffering, like Amy Carmichael, or to grope through the last chapter blind, like Ira D. Sankey. No vision of angels, no last days of glorious homegoing, perchance a weird departure in a great *why?* If it be so and we murmur, "Why is my soul troubled and what shall I say?" then let us pray what our Lord said when he uttered those words, "Father, glorify Thy Name!"

At this writing I am in the third segment of this fourfold prayer. My Lord has not come and I have not gone. Either of the four possibilities may turn real tomorrow. I do not choose; I do not have an option though I may have a wish. All four are in my Father's hand. Who dares to say that life cannot be interesting when every day holds all these experiences in the "could-be's" of tomorrow . . . or even now!

Come what may, let us trust and not be afraid. His will never leads us where His grace cannot keep us.

4

God and the Odd Sparrow

In Matthew our Lord spoke of two sparrows sold for a farthing and in Luke we read of five sparrows for two farthings. The second deal is a bargain with one sparrow thrown in extra. Our Lord made it plain that God knows about and cares for the most insignificant things.

There are sparrows and sparrows. I love to listen to the white-throated variety with that song that begins like the "Wedding March" lifted octaves beyond human reach. Also the song sparrow, so cheerful almost the year round. The field sparrow brings back memories of my boyhood on the little farm when on a desperately hot day while I was hoeing all other birds kept a sweltering silence. But not the field sparrow. He could be heard singing gaily in the hottest weather like a chickadee in the coldest winter.

But the English sparrow is the commonest of the breed, a visitor from overseas who has multiplied beyond any others in the clan. He is a town bird and has many of the same characteristics of town people amidst the hubbub of the traffic. He cannot sing; he only chirps monotonously all day. Other sparrows would never be caught in a city but the English sparrow seems to the manner born. He and his counterparts are found in many lands.

The Psalmist mourned that he was as a sparrow alone upon the housetop. Sparrows are gregarious and not solitary but we are told that when the nest is destroyed or the mate is lost the survivor may be observed in loneliness and disconsolation.

What did our Lord mean when He said that the sparrow

does not fall without our Father's notice? The cynic may say, "But the sparrow falls just the same. We see them lying around almost any day. Small comfort that!" But there is something deeper than meets the eye in this precious word. In this universe everything is known to God even to the slightest detail. Nothing ever becomes actually nonexistent. It is a law of nature and any scientist can tell you that things change form but never cease to be. The burning wood goes up in smoke and is reduced to ashes but its component elements are still around.

With the child of God no prayer, no tear, nothing is lost. All things work together for good to him in the purpose of God. The hairs of our head are numbered. We do not lose our dear ones by death. If they are the Lord's they are with Him and in His sight all live somewhere. The unbeliever is lost by choice if he is not found in the family of God, but he still exists and hell is the garbage heap where the worm dies not and the fire is not quenched.

God knows what He has in stock in His universe and no item, however small, is unknown to Him. One day in the final restoration of all things we are going to see all things that puzzle us now fitted into a complete picture. Everybody and everything will be where they belong. There will be no odd pieces, no meaningless rubbish. And everyone in heaven, on earth and under the earth shall confess that Jesus is Lord. That will not mean universal salvation but it does mean that everybody and everything will be accounted for. God will overlook nothing. How good to know that "His eye is on the sparrow and I know He watches me!"

5

That Vacant Stare

Back from a bit of supper in a motel restaurant, a routine that has become almost automatic in nearly forty years on the road. I've done it until I'm almost a manikin; the food tastes the same to this robot. There's a difference from the way it used to be. Sara has been gone for years and I find myself sitting in my side of that restaurant booth staring straight ahead at where she used to be. It is a vacant stare of course for she isn't there and I know it. (Sometimes I wonder—does she ever hover near?)

Actually we never have seen each other. We see the body, but that spirit, soul or whatever you want to call it that looked through those eyes, heard with those ears, spoke with that tongue, that was the true Sara and I never saw her. You can see a brain but not a mind. One day the body is laid away, ashes to ashes, dust to dust, but not the tenant of that tenement.

The Bible tells me that my dear one's spirit is with Jesus. There is a lot we don't understand as yet about that. Do these dear ones now have some form of manifestation before they get their resurrection bodies? Alexander Maclaren says that if God can localize a spirit in a body He can localize a spirit without a body! One thing I know, one day my stare will not be vacant! I am looking straight ahead and not in vain. Sometime, somewhere ahead, I will see no longer through a glass as in a riddle. Now I know in part but then I shall know even as I am known. "Now" will become "then." We are not the Saints of the Blank Look. Faith will give way to sight. I have never seen my Lord but daily I am "off-looking unto Him" until we

meet. Though now I see Him not, "yet believing, (I) rejoice
with joy unspeakable and full of glory." It is not a vacant stare
after all. It is an eager peering through the fog; it is anticipation, expectation, traveling on until the mists have rolled away.

An old father was waiting for his son's return from the war.
He was to get home the next day. On the day before he asked a
friend,

"Have you seen my John?"

"No, is he home?"

"Coming tomorrow!"

Carried away with anticipation he was a little ahead of himself! We are like that. We may be pardoned if, since it is all as
good as done, we sing and speak as though it would all happen
tomorrow. Why not? Perhaps today!

I am not staring blankly at a wall in the motel restaurant.
They call us the Saints of the Vacant Look but they don't understand. What God says will be is a sure thing and only a little
time lies between any of it and us. We see not the temporal but
the eternal while we look not at the seen but the unseen. Distance and time mean little to the soul that walks with Him who
never *was* but forever Is, the Great I Am.

You are not looking at a wall, dear heart. It looks like it but
one day the trumpet will sound and Jericho will tumble and we
shall possess the land.

> We shall meet again,
> How sweet the time will be.

It's as good as done. Let not the Evil One laugh at you and
discourage your hope. The last laugh will be God's and yours.
Keep looking straight ahead and walk as you look. It won't be
long.

6

Time Out

A South Carolina friend told me about meeting a typical old Southern gentleman who said, "I used to come over to your town quite often in the old days. It was a day's round trip by horse and buggy. I can do it now in an hour but I don't have time!" That just about sums up the tempo—and the tragedy—of these hurried times. I noticed recently that one of our church hymnals no longer carries the precious song, "Take Time To Be Holy." Who's got time to be holy? We've got a program we must put over! And time is one thing it does take to be holy. When we're too busy for that we're too busy.

We have never lived so close together—and so far apart. Up and down the country road of my boyhood days lived my farming neighbors. Now they are commuters who work in town and they do not have time to get acquainted. During the revival at old Corinth Church in the summertime we visited each other, sat on the veranda or piazza (remember those old words?), ate watermelon and just talked. No use visiting now. They're all out in their cars or if you should catch them at home you can't out-talk television. Home-wise, the whole country is a disaster area from Maine to California. Some fine exceptions manage to survive and they ought to be decorated for bucking such a tide.

Nobody wants to go back to dirt roads, kerosene lamps and the early Fords. But if ever we threw out the baby with the bathwater we did it this time. When we gave up these symbols of earlier days somehow we also gave up time to think, to reflect, to meditate, to watch a sunset, to hear a bird song. I am with a different preacher almost every week and few have time for a walk. There's a committee meeting right away or the Sons and Daughters of I Will Arise are having a supper and he must be there. The last man who had time to talk was John Brown, a farmer in my first pastorate. We spent many an hour just talking when he should have been plowing and I should have been visiting. He came to my room and we sat up late typing some of his poems. One night we sat up with a sick man and talked in a low voice from dark to daylight.

My father always went from the supper table to sit alone on the back porch and look at the mountains in the distance— Table Rock, Grandfather and the rest of them while he pondered his past, present and future. He allowed nothing to cheat him out of that escape from things as they were. If any modern Isaac chose to meditate in the fields at eventide these days this generation would conclude that the old boy was off his rocker.

At long last some Americans are beginning to come to. The transcendentalists are meditating, Uncle Sam talks physical fitness, and the joggers have hit the road. (Have you heard of the poor fellow who dropped dead recently jogging home from a health food store?)

But you can't jog and meditate at the same time. All you can do is puff and blow. God ordained walking, the perfect exercise; but walking is still an un-American activity. If you see somebody strolling along a highway actually thinking, you pronounce him out of his head or out of gas. We've been years developing our present life-style and life-styles are not changed by occasional spurts of trying to get back to Thoreau's Pond. Or taking off in a new camper for some national park where you look out the window at the fellow in the next camper to yours who has driven two thousand miles to get away from it all and found himself with two thousand more refugees from progress who've brought it all with them just as you have done. The main trouble is we've brought ourselves along. Escaping from that character is difficult business. It means getting through to God and being regenerated. It is to be hoped that we don't end up merely with a new fad of born-again-ism instead of getting into the gait of Galilee with Jesus Christ.

7

Why?

One of the words most often on the lips of youngsters is that little three-letter question, "Why?" Any parent knows what it is to be bombarded all day by an inquiring tyke with a barrage of "Whys." We never get over it as we grow up. We see the trouble and the tragedy, the misery and the mystery, the iniquities and the inequities of life and so much of it doesn't add up or make sense. And we sometimes wonder, "Where is God?"

Like Job we moan, "Oh that I knew where I might find him! . . . I go forward, but he is not there; and backward, but I cannot perceive him: on the left hand, where he doth work, but I cannot behold him: he hideth himself on the right hand, that I cannot see him." Like the Psalmist we complain, "O God, why hast thou cast us off forever? why doth thine anger smoke against the sheep of thy pasture?" With Jeremiah we ask, "Why is my pain perpetual, and my wound incurable, which refuseth to be healed? wilt thou be altogether unto me as a liar, and as waters that fail?"

If you have visited a hospital for crippled, retarded, abnormal children, their little bodies twisted, grotesque, sometimes hideous; if you have visited a home for the aged and have beheld those pitiful vegetables, kept alive sometimes by machines that prolong death and not life, shapeless lumps of flesh unable to live or die; if you have walked in cemeteries where lie the bodies of countless soldiers, boys who died, some of them in vain; if you have looked on victims of hurricane, flood and fire or the corpses of innocent men and women murdered by maniacs; if you have watched the haunting faces of alcoholics, drug addicts, the despair of terminal illness; if you have held the hand of a dying dear one as I have done whom physicians and prayer alike had failed to save . . . if you have faced the ironic enigmas that add up to nothing in your arithmetic, if dreams have been blasted and hopes destroyed by the heartless law of cause and effect with no answer from brazen heavens, your heart may cry out with the biggest little word in your vocabulary, "My God, WHY?"

So we make our way through a mass and a mess of unanswered questions with no possible answer until we have better light. Everything is mixed up, one day a precious answer to prayer, next day some weird calamity. One day, miracle; the next day, misery, and it adds up to mystery, like the weather with sunny skies and singing birds followed by storm and destruction. There is no discernible orderly weather pattern because even the weather was fouled up by the fall of man. And life is like the weather, without rhyme or reason, so much that happens because of the havoc wrought by sin and Satan.

But we need not bombard heaven with our "Whys" because God has answered all our agony and distress in one all-inclusive "Why." We can never fathom the depths of that "Why," but we can rest in the certainty that in it is found the meaning of all our troubles and the fulfillment of every shattered dream. It is the cry of Jesus Christ on the cross, "My God, my God, why hast thou forsaken me?" When that "Why" was uttered the greatest thing that ever happened in all history was taking place. It is beyond our understanding for if our poor minds could explain it, there wouldn't be much to it. And if we could understand it we wouldn't need faith. But there it is, the WHY of all WHYS that gathers up all the others and answers them forever.

8

"God Forsaken of God"

The writer of the twenty-second Psalm gave us a description of the crucifixion centuries before Jesus died on the cross. When we remember that crucifixion was a Roman way of execution, not a Jewish, only divine inspiration can account for a Hebrew writing centuries in advance a word picture of Calvary. He gives the details: bones out of joint (v. 14), agony (vv. 14, 15), thirst (v. 15), partial nudity and scorn (vv. 7, 8, 17), casting lots (v. 18). All of this was fulfilled precisely and our Lord climaxed the torture by crying out the first verse of this Psalm, "My God, my God, why hast thou forsaken me?"

What does all this mean? The Psalm is the cry of the Psalmist, the cry of a man and of men who feel forsaken of God. You hear it often in varied forms. "Why doesn't God do something?" One thinks of the disciples in the storm-tossed boat on Galilee: "Carest thou not that we perish?" Why doesn't God break through the reign of cause and effect and intervene in all this mess? If He is omniscient He knows all about it and if He is omnipotent He can do something about it. If Psalm 22 stopped there, without any follow-up, life would indeed be a tale told by a fool, full of sound and fury, signifying nothing. We would be only the victims of a demonic monster and humanity simply a mass of impure carbohydrates headed for oblivion.

But centuries after Psalm 22 was written, the Son of God screamed that first verse on Calvary. It came at the end of the most awful six hours in history between 9:00 A.M. and 3:00 P.M. when everything turned dark, when God turned off the light while His Son was dying in the dark. God who cannot look upon sin turned His back while His Son drank the dregs of that cup of all the sins of all men of all time in order that God might be Just and Justifier, that the judgment seat might become the mercy seat, that God might be propitiated and sinners reconciled.

> Well might the sun in darkness hide
> And shut his glories in,
> When Christ, the mighty Marker died
> For man the creature's sin.

What an hour! Luther pondered it all alone and at great length while he fasted, and finally arose to say, "God forsaken of God . . . who can understand it!" There are heathen records of an eclipse of the sun at that time. Diogenes witnessed an eclipse and darkness in Egypt and said, "Either the Deity himself suffers at this moment or sympathizes with someone who does."

And never forget that while religionists reviled and ridiculed the suffering Saviour, a Roman centurion who had never heard a sermon perhaps and had never been in a revival observed, "Truly this was the Son of God."

God's Son with no sin in Him became our sin with all sin upon Him. This was why He came to earth to begin with. In spite of learned divines who conjecture that He simply came to start a movement and when it failed He had to die, He himself declared that He came to seek and to save the lost and to give His life as a ransom for many. Prophecy and sacrifice in the Old Testament proclaim it and throughout His public ministry, "Mine hour" was constantly on His mind. We cannot understand.

"God forsaken of God" . . . it will take all eternity to fathom that!

9

Why Did He Die?

We have dressed up Calvary in theological gobbledygook or sickly sentimentality so as not to offend fastidious church-goers who do not want to be disturbed by gory references to a bruised, beaten, bleeding Saviour, His beard pulled out and face covered with spittle, dying between two thieves. There is nothing elegant about that sight. I know an artist who paints pictures of Gethsemane and Golgotha. They are not pretty pictures. The artist is disturbed by pictures that do not disturb us, pictures that give the impression that our Lord is only experiencing some minor inconvenience. Jesus walked on earth as a man but on the cross He poured out His soul unto death and suffered only as God can suffer. Many people have been crucified. The agony of Calvary was not limited to physical suffering. That alone is beyond words for there is no more awful way to die than by crucifixion. But this is the heartbreak of God.

Why did my Lord die? In one sense, He did not have to die. We die because we have to. The wages of sin is death but Jesus never sinned and so had no debt to pay for Himself. He could lay down His life and take it up again. We can lay down our lives, we can kill ourselves, but we cannot take up our lives again. On the way to Calvary, Jesus said to weeping women, "Weep not for me." He was not the helpless victim of a mob. He was dying on purpose. He told Peter He could call down twelve legions of angels and reminded Pilate that He had no power except it were given Him from above. He was in complete charge of His own death. He prayed for those who cruci-

fied Him, arranged for John to keep His mother, and gave the
dying thief a ticket to Paradise. Then He turned His spirit over
to God. He was in full command of the situation, in possession
of His faculties. No man ever lived as this man. No man ever
died like this man.

In a sense He did not have to die, but He also did have to
die. Only God could meet the demands of God's righteousness
and only a man could identify with sinful humanity. As God-
Man, Jesus Christ did both. But you say, "We still sin and suffer and die." When Jesus died it looked as if it was all over
with Him and that He was finished. But three days later He
arose, forty days later He went back to heaven, and He is coming again. All who trust Him will be changed and reign with
Him forever. Everything is finished in the plan and purpose of
God but we are in the middle of the book of that purpose and
final fulfillment has yet to come.

When He comes all our "Whys" will be answered, but not in
a question-and-answer show. "In that day ye shall ask me
nothing."

All the "Whys," the problems and heartaches, the sin and
sorrow and suffering, the unanswered miseries and mysteries of
today have been wrapped up and taken care of in those awful
six hours on the cross. But all would have been lost if the angel
had not opened that tomb three days later and if he had not sat
upon it to make clear who was in command around there! Our
preaching is the message of the cross and God forbid that we
preach less than Christ crucified for our sins and raised for our
justification. Something was finished at Calvary but three days
later something else was begun. There is a finished work of
Christ but there is also an unfinished work of Christ and we
had better be about the proclamation and living today of all
that Jesus began to do and to teach.

10

When the Future Looks Dark

Among my souvenirs I treasure a scrapbook of precious items. In that scrapbook are two pages that face each other, with two brief inscriptions. The left hand page bears a barely legible line by my dear Sara in her last illness. It looked as though, if she recovered at all, it might be to face life as an invalid. She had managed to scribble, "My future looks dark." But God spared her such a finish by taking her to Himself where everything is bright forever.

On the opposite page, Sara's mother—we called her "Mammaw"—had written on a birthday card those blessed lines, "What looks dark in the distance will brighten as we draw near." It is the outlook answered by the uplook. Those two dear ones have preceded us now and already they know more about that other world than all the theologians.

I spoke at the funeral of my own mother years ago. The last message she sent to me in Michigan was dictated to my brother as he wrote a letter: "Tell Vance to keep up the good fight, for God is with him, and if God be for us who can be against us!" I am thankful for a mother and a mother-in-law who believed firmly in heaven, the Land of the Uncloudy Day, the Land of No More—no more sorrow, no more death, and no more night. I do not like darkness. I dread to see it come and I get up at an unearthly hour to watch it depart. I feel like helping the sun climb over the horizon.

To everybody there come those times when the future looks dark.

> Into each life some rain must fall
> Some days must be dark and dreary.

But to the soul "that on Jesus hath leaned for repose" it just *looks* that way. Now we see through a glass as in a riddle but one day the riddle will become reality. If the future looks dark, remember you are seeing it *from here*. We do not yet see all things in submission to Him, but "we see Jesus."

Ira D. Sankey, whose gospel singing blessed the multitudes in the days of Moody, went blind in his later years. One day a visitor asked him, "Do you still play the little organ and sing?" Mr. Sankey got up, felt his way to the organ and began to sing and play,

> There'll be no dark valley when Jesus comes
> To gather His loved ones home.

If all our departed Christian loved ones could speak from that cloud of witnesses that holds us in full survey (and there are so many more over there than there are over here!) they would bid us onward, for

> What looks dark in the distance
> will brighten as we draw near.

11

Among My Souvenirs

Pictures, clippings, and trinkets accumulate as the years go by, and when almost eighty of those years have added to the collection, a lot of heartthrobs and memories gather with them. One of my prizes is an old country newspaper ready to fall apart. The year is 1915 and it is full of curiosities and a show window to a life-style now forgotten. One is an advertisement announcing a Fourth of July celebration in a tiny town called Hollis. Three attractions are presented: free lemonade, a balloon ascension and Vance Havner, the boy preacher! I was thirteen then and for over a year had been preaching here and there at town and country churches, usually just one sermon at a place and on Sundays. This was an extra occasion. I stood in a wagon outdoors in a ravine while a little natural amphitheater rose around me. I wore a new white suit my Dad had bought for me, short knee pants and all. Curiosity brought a crowd and they came not only to see and hear me but to drink the free lemonade and see the balloon go up. I can remember very little about the sermon, my feelings or the response of the crowd. Dad was somewhat bewildered at having a preaching thirteen-year-old son.

He had been called to preach but never became a preacher. Of course his soul delighted in my early start but he did not make a preacher out of me. I never knew the day when I did not feel that I should preach. Father had two preacher brothers, one a Baptist and one a Methodist. He was a faithful Christian and was devoted to old Corinth Baptist Church up the road a mile from where I grew up. He tried to do well the next best thing, but all his life he regretted that he did not preach.

Another precious souvenir in my collection is a faded old letter from Dad sent to me in 1919 when I was attending college. He wrote, "Be at your very best in everything for I am hoping for great things from you in the by and by." It is "by and by" now and this finds that son eighty with sixty-eight years of preaching behind him and thirty-one books. Yet I am somewhat bewildered at it all. I can only praise God and sing, "All the way my Saviour leads me, what have I to ask beside?" Father missed his calling and could have been a great blessing because I believe he would have been an able preacher. I almost missed my way for a while but returned to the old message after some unsettled years in the late teens and early twenties. Father was uneasy then and passed away at sixty but I feel that he sees and knows and we'll talk it over in the final and eternal by and by.

I have often thought that Naaman would have missed his miracle if he had not washed in Jordan. The blind man with the anointed eyes would have missed his miracle if he had not headed for the Pool of Siloam. And Philip would have missed his miracle if he had not gone down that desert road as God commanded. Have you missed your miracle, the blessing God had for you? The disobedient prophet did it when he stopped over to eat after God had given him other orders. King Saul did it in his stubbornness. And the rich young ruler missed it when he made the Great Refusal.

Nothing else can be as good as the blessing God has for you.

12

On Not Getting "With It"

It was long ago that a very energetic and successful Christian brother advised me to snap out of my slow countrified gait and "get with it" in the new stepped-up pattern of modern Christian work. He didn't put it just that way but to him my lifestyle was a carry-over from the horse-and-buggy era and needed updating. I knew what he meant. I should organize an "association" or a "foundation," a sponsoring board, set up an office with a secretary, get on radio maybe, promote my preaching and writing with brochures. (Somehow I thought of the brothers of Jesus urging Him to go up to Jerusalem and perform before the public, forsake the backwoods for the boulevards. The gait of Galilee irritated them. He had only three years and ... well, if He'd only get going, maybe with His miracles and all, He might "make" Alexandria, Athens, Rome!)

Somehow my friend's advice didn't "take." I am still operating on a shoestring, as they say. No office, no study, no secretary. Never dictated a letter. Typed out thirty-two books all by myself. No "foundation" except the one "laid for (my) faith in His excellent Word." Never had a regular radio program. Never owed but two hundred dollars in my life. I borrowed it as a youth going to school. My father said that dirt, debt and the devil were related so I decided to keep away from all three as far as possible. I've not been on drugs or in jail and have no sensational stories to tell of an awful past. It is characteristic of a sick generation that to tell of God's leading from boyhood does not make "news." Healing miracles make good copy but why does a story of good health for most of a century leave the audience bored? With me there has been little that is dramatic, glamorous, Hollywood. Just plain vanilla. I'm still just "preaching and writing" but God has blessed it beyond my fondest dreams.

I'm not criticizing those who do it the other way. For them it may be best and God blesses them too. Remember, I'm telling *my* story. Now at eighty I'm glad I kept it simple. There are more open doors than I can enter and God has blessed the little books and given me a multitude of listeners and readers at home and abroad. He has been Promoter, Advance Agent, Secretary and Treasurer. He took me into partnership long ago. The pay may seem small to some but the retirement benefits are "out of this world!" All this and heaven too! "In all thy ways acknowledge him, and he shall direct thy paths." His business is guaranteed. The vaults of heaven are moth-proof, rust-proof and thief-proof. His eyes run to and fro throughout the earth to show himself strong in our behalf, not to show us strong in His behalf. You don't have to get with *it,* you only have to get with *Him!*

13

Another Christmas

It's Christmas Eve again and the eighth Christmas since my Sara went away. I am reminded of what Dr. R. G. Lee said as we stood in his home before the large picture of Lady Lee: "And it doesn't get any easier."

Maybe I'm too sentimental and old-fashioned these days when the Good Book says people will be "without natural affection." Those words have many applications but I feel that millions today are incapable of ordinary human love. Therefore marriage is on the skids and a pertinent question for millions would be, "Is there a *home* in your *house?*" A multitude nowadays live together as man and wife without bothering to get married. Others have such a cheap and heartless love that they soon part company and don't miss their companions when death separates them. Even among nice folks second marriages happen so soon that when I meet a recent widower with a new lady friend amazingly soon after the funeral I do not know whether to console the bereaved or congratulate the new groom.

To me, Sara was not the soon-forgotten sort. Thirty-three years of her companionship are not a faded memory already. I was a lonely soul for thirty-nine years before I found my dear lady and now eight more milestones of loneliness mark her departure. This Christmas I got out the tiny Christmas tree about which I have written before. I've hung a few wreaths and brightened up the breakfast room with a little red and green. But if I had a house full of Christmas beauty I'd give it all to see for a moment a familiar figure come in the door in that red robe and greet me as of old.

But the separation is only momentary as we look beyond the sunset to glad reunion with those dear ones who've gone before. God has been so good to me. Many preachers retire at sixty-five but I have already had sixty-eight years in the ministry itself. God has given me the desires of my heart and I cannot complain after such a full life. All the way my Saviour has led me . . . what have I to ask beside?

Soon I'll be back on the road again, back to motel living and returning at night where I go after the meetings to face the wall with no one to talk things over. No human dear one, that is, and how Adam does have need of Eve! But there is One whose presence I doubt not and "though now we see him not, *yet believing,* we rejoice with joy unspeakable and full of glory." I have learned to weep with those who weep and give a word of comfort to the loneliest generation that has ever come along.

Somehow the Christmas season is always the most difficult for lonely souls; even youth today are beset with loneliness and have set up a suicide record of their own. All the brain-boggling wonders of our modern technology with its computer marvels, and now robots! . . . leave us bored and managing only a "So what?" Christmas has almost been lost in a money-mad orgy where there is performance but not much experience.

> O holy Child of Bethlehem . . .
> BE BORN IN US TODAY!

14

Falling Leaves

I've been over in the woods. How good it is in these frantic, insane times—the age of the superficial and the artificial, performing mind-boggling tricks of science but with the morals of an alley cat—how good it is to slip away from TV and traffic just a few moments to where things don't change much, where they are pretty much like they have always been!

It is November and "the melancholy days have come, the saddest of the year," the farewell of summer and the falling leaves. All season long they have waved their little flags but now they are dying and lovelier in death than in life, decked now in robes of splendor. What with winter ahead and a long way to spring, I am not feeling my gayest. But autumn is not without its message of hope. Soon the falling leaves will disintegrate on the breast of Mother Earth. But give a few months and the show starts all over. I'll be walking along in the naked woods and, lo, there is a bit of green peeping out. The smallest spring bud is as welcome as a spring in the desert. Then the "red, red robin" will be "bob, bob, bobbin' along" and the warblers will take over the trees.

Sometimes I feel like the last leaf on the tree of my generation. So many old friends are gone, old acquaintances forgotten and departed. But not forever. Resurrection is ahead, as sure as violets in springtime. We shall live again. "Life is ever lord of death and love can never lose its own." We live in a universe of mystery with a thousand "Whys" but "the Lord God omnipotent reigneth." Everybody and everything will end up where they belong. The sparrow does not fall without His notice. If winter comes, can spring be far behind?

If the autumn leaves bid us goodbye in their brightest colors, we need not take leave of this world in drab array. True, our bodies may not look their best by then. When our Lord was laid away He was scarcely recognizable. But do not confuse the tenant with the tenement. We pin the first violet on our lapel when spring arrives. Why not a gorgeous leaf from autumn? Both symbolize precious seasons and should bedeck the mind and heart with what they say. Even cold and barren winter is really no meaningless waiting spell even though we may sometimes wish we could hibernate after leaving orders to wake us up in April. Winter is busy as can be getting things in order for the next chapter. Falling leaves should bring a song along with the sigh.

15

Jesus Is Not an Additive

The word "additive" is getting a lot of usage these days. It means, of course, something added to something else, usually to improve or strengthen. It is fashionable to call God in for special occasions, political campaigns, ball games, business advantages (being a church member may help one's prestige in some quarters and it always looks good in an obituary).

Jesus Christ is not on call to help lend an aura to human endeavor, an extra plus to our education, personality, prestige. Nicodemus made the mistake of thinking that if he could add what Jesus could give to all he already had as a master of Israel he would have it made. But Jesus added in effect, "I am not a new page in your book. You must begin a new book by being born again!"

The rich young ruler wanted to add eternal life to his many possessions but the Saviour told him that he had to sell out all he had to begin with. The prospective disciples in the ninth chapter of Luke put Jesus NEXT, after burying a father and telling a family goodbye FIRST. But Jesus Christ never comes next. He does not play second fiddle. He is Alpha and Omega, the first and the last. He said "Seek ye first the kingdom of God, and his righteousness; and all these things shall be added unto you." There is where the additives belong, after the first comes first. The prospective disciple said, "Permit me first." Our Lord said "Seek ye first." It is a matter of priorities.

Gamaliel compared the cause of Christ with Theudas and Judas, rabble-rousers of the past. But Jesus Christ is Jesus Christ.

No mortal can with Him compare
Among the sons of men;
Fairer is He than all the fair
Who fill the heavenly train.

This prevalent idea that one's relationship to Jesus Christ can be put anywhere on the totem pole of our concerns is a lot of eyewash. By Him all things consist and the Christian should say, "To me to live is Christ." He is not just Item One in life's interests; He includes all the rest of them in Himself. The average church member today makes his religious life a matter of mere church membership with a few occasional observances and donations. He agrees that "religion" is important and necessary but Jesus is simply one of his many concerns instead of being the Christ of all his concerns, Lord of all he is and has and does. Such a casual Christianity is not even a distant relative of the original brand. Jesus was not an additive to that original band; He was everything and for Him they lived and died. He was Beginning and End and everything else found its place between that Alpha and Omega.

You do not add Him to what you already have. The word "Christian" ends with IAN and that stands for "I Am Nothing." We are zeros until we relate to Him. Sometime ago I received a check that should have been for one thousand dollars but a typing mistake had added a zero and made it ten thousand! Zeros have no value, no matter how many they are, unless they follow a numeral. Beside Jesus Christ we take on value, but He does not come NEXT.

16

Reflections of a Bird Watcher

I have been an ardent bird watcher since my boyhood. It began when I started collecting bird cards from baking soda boxes. Mother sent me up the country road to the little grocery store to trade a few eggs for a few groceries—including baking soda—and I always hoped there would be a few pennies change which I might use to buy some sticks of candy.

As time went on I bought bird guides, binoculars, bird song recordings. I set out to see how many feathered songsters I could learn to identify by sight or sound. Through the years it has been a fascinating pursuit and now I can recognize a fairly good number of these performers. It can be an exasperating business. After hours of following an elusive warbler, and just when I almost see him, he takes off for parts unknown.

Bird watching has taught me a precious lesson. For a while I was bent on being able to check any bird in the bird guide for that area. I got into an exhausting pursuit of new species instead of enjoying the birds I did know. I will never be a Roger Tory Peterson nor will I master the singing birds alone, to say nothing of water birds, game birds or birds of prey. Now and then I add a new discovery to the seen and heard songsters I have heard and known. But I have not grimly set my face to make a complete score. I am glad when once in a while I strike a new acquaintance but I am enjoying what I see and hear now.

I read about one avid bird watcher who set his goal at so many new birds last year. Someone would call in from the other side of the country to report a new bird and this dear man would jump into his private plane and cross the continent to see that bird. I am not that interested in new birds.

The application of this principle spills over into all realms of life. It holds in Christian living. There is no contradiction between hungering and thirsting after righteousness and the other blessed truth that he who drinks the Living Water shall never thirst. There is the sad mistake of feeding on devotional books and chasing one Bible teacher after another without living daily as much of that life as we already know. There is such a thing as setting out grimly to live a maximum Christian life instead of enjoying daily the grace that is ours *now*. We never learn it all so let us make much of our present experience. It is poor business to be so dead set on learning a new bird every day that we do not hear the wood thrush today. One can make a closer walk with God tomorrow his goal so ardently that he does not walk with Him today.

I am going to enjoy the birds I hear now. A bird in the hand is worth more than a bird in the bush tomorrow. The yellow throat along the creek, the warblers in the treetops, the tanagers and vireos, the little ovenbird in the woods—I shall listen to them, and if no strange new voice is heard I will not let that spoil the day. I will enjoy God's grace now and not lose the blessedness of climbing just because I have not reached a desired summit. Let us make the most of ground already gained while we press on to higher ground ahead.

17

"Jesus Is Gonna Win"

The old bootblack in the barber shop was a familiar figure with his Bible always lying close at hand when he was not reading it. One day a customer said to him, "I see you're reading the Book of Revelation today. Do you understand it?"

"Yes, sir, I know what it means."

"You know what it means when Bible scholars have disagreed about it all these years! What do you think it means?"

"It means that Jesus is gonna win!"

I doubt that a theologian could come up with a better summary of what the Apocalypse means. That book is the most amazing scenario of future events ever written in eye-dazzling colors and mind-boggling grandeur. In its wildest moments Hollywood can never match the horrors and glories that will one day become a visible pageant, making our mightiest drama look like a kindergarten operetta. Beasts and seals, scorpions and dragons, Babylon and the 666, Gog and Magog, earthquakes and falling stars, the downfall of the devil, the Great White City, the River of Life and Jesus Christ on His throne with every knee bowing and heaven triumphant over hell. "Jesus is gonna win!"

When times are good and we are in health Revelation is little read and not thought worthy of our attention. But when the storm breaks and the winds shake the curtains of our temporary dwelling place, this blessed word from God grows more precious than any earthly treasure. Jesus is going to win because He has already won at Calvary and the open grave. But we do not yet see all things put under Him as we await His ultimate triumph. Our Waterloo has already been fought, what we are now engaged in are the mopping-up exercises!

When Jesus was here on earth it looked as though He could not possibly win. When they took His battered body down from that cross, His visage so marred that He scarcely resembled a man, He looked like the greatest loser of all time. But although the powers of evil blocked his sepulcher with a massive stone and put their seal on it, a mighty angel broke the seal, rolled back the stone and sat upon it as if to say, "Now look who's in charge around here!" That started the biggest Win of all time and eternity.

That final and everlasting victory is assured though the saints of God have often marched through blood and tears throughout the centuries. We have sung it when we saw few signs of it and rested our weary heads many a night on tear-stained pillows because God said it and we believe it—JESUS IS GONNA WIN!

Look not to symposiums on TV shows where learned experts pool their ignorance. Seek not your solace from mortal men who, however brilliant in their heads, cannot receive the things of the Spirit of God until their hearts are changed. These things have been kept from the wise and prudent and revealed unto babes. A bootblack in a barber shop may have understanding of the times to know what we ought to do while some PhDs grope in darkness. We have better light on where we are and where we are going than will ever come from a panel of news analysts. We've had it for almost two thousand years in a little book that says "JESUS IS GONNA WIN!"

18

When the Dam Breaks

Not long ago I preached for some days at the Toccoa Falls Bible College in Georgia where, a few years before, a frightful dam break took thirty-nine lives and wreaked appalling destruction. An investigator from Washington visited the scene to assess the damage. Of course many would need to rebuild and make a new start. The greatest loss in missing loved ones could never be replaced. But the Christians of that little community rose to the occasion and demonstrated a faith that did not need treatment for shock, panic, or emotional collapse. Somebody said, "They've got something else!"

Jeremiah wrote to the people of his land, beset with adversaries and facing greater foes ahead: "If thou hast run with the footmen, and they have wearied thee, then how canst thou contend with horses? and if in the land of peace, wherein thou trustedst, they wearied thee, then how wilt thou do in the swelling of Jordan?" In other words, "If little problems get you down, what will you do when big trouble comes?"

The dam is breaking in America. Unless there is a spiritual revival, we might as well try to hold back Niagara Falls with toothpicks. The restraints of law and order are giving way. Our family life is crumbling. Ours is a day of secularism and humanism which has been defined as "the practice of the absence of God." With our technology, know-how and expertise, we are producing brain-boggling gadgets but the real problem is sin, and science has no answer to sin.

When the dam broke in Toccoa Falls, it was natural law on a rampage but the Christian citizens did not go to pieces. *"They had something else*"—better still "Someone else." We have only two options today, Christ or chaos. God began with law and order but the devil got into the garden and Adam and Eve ate us out of house and home. The dam is breaking today and humanity needs more than disaster relief. We need a Rock in a weary land, a shelter in time of storm.

What will you do in the swelling of Jordan? You may reach old age in good health with your children around you. Or tragedy may come, bereavement, that accident that makes no sense, that calamity you can't add up on your little computer. The doctor may say, "It's cancer." You may run into business trouble, family trouble or years in a retirement home, unloved and unvisited. Anything can happen, but are we ready? Jesus said, "In the world ye shall have tribulation: but be of good cheer; I have overcome the world." He said, "Lo, I am with you all the days." Then, no matter what the day brings forth, you won't need a psychiatrist or a shot of sedative. You'll have something else. You'll have SOMEONE else, if you trust and obey Him.

He does not walk with us visibly these days. But He told us the Holy Spirit would come to be our Helper. Don't try to figure out all the theology of that. The Spirit has not come to supersede Jesus but to testify of Him and make Him more real. And He will guide you into all truth. And be with you in every situation.

Even if the dam breaks.

19

The Groaning Creation

Two travelers were camping on the edge of a great desert. In the middle of the night one aroused his companion to ask "What is that moaning sound I hear?" The other replied, "That is the desert sighing."

We live in a *groaning world.* "The whole creation groaneth and travaileth in pain together until now" (Rom. 8:22). When God created the earth it was good in His sight. Every prospect was pleasing and not even man was vile. The weather was perfect, the lion and the lamb were at peace, Adam and Eve lived happily but not ever after for Satan came on the scene, evil appeared and sin began. Today we live in a ruined world, still beautiful in spots but groaning in pain. The creatures live under the law of tooth and claw and pretty pictures in nature books do not tell the whole story.

If you are sensitive to the voices of nature you can detect the sigh and the groan. Goethe wrote, "Often have I had the sensation as if nature in wailing sadness entreated something of me so that not to understand what was longed for cut to heart." Dr. A. T. Robertson wrote, "The mystical sympathy of physical nature with the work of grace is beyond comprehension to most of us but who can disprove it?" And John Keble wrote:

> It was not then a poet's dream,
> An idle vaunt of song,
> Which bids me see in heaven or earth
> In all things fair around
> Strong yearnings for a blest new birth
> With sinless glories crowned.

The groan and the glory! Have you not sensed it in some favored spot? Some of us call it the whisper of the "earnest expectation of the creature (waiting) for the manifestation of the
sons of God." The groan that longs for the glory!

There is far more agony than ecstasy in this world of things
as they are. Visit a children's hospital, a home for the aged, a
bedside of terminal illness. Or Arlington Cemetery, or
Flanders fields where "poppies blow between the crosses, row
on row." Even teen-agers are not immune to the groan or else
they would not run up such suicide records. In the face of the
trouble and tragedy, the misery and the mystery, the iniquities
and inequities of life, so much doesn't add up on our little
computers. Life is so often like the weather, without rhyme or
reason. One thinks of Job crying, "Oh that I knew where I
might find him! . . . I go forward, but he is not there; and backward, but I cannot perceive Him: on the left hand, where he
doth work, but . . . he hideth himself on the right hand, that I
cannot see him" (Job 23:2, 8, 9).

That little word "Why?" is on our lips and in our minds
from childhood. In the midst of a groaning creation "My God,
why?" is our constant refrain. The Psalmist raised it centuries
ago and it was answered by the dying Saviour with that all-inclusive "Why" that gathers up in itself the meaning of all the
"Whys" of history. For into a *groaning creation* came the
groaning Christ.

20

The Groaning Christ

More is wrapped up than the eye can see in that blessed description of Jesus as "Man of sorrows and acquainted with grief." At the grave of Lazarus He was troubled in spirit and wept. A. T. Robertson says that in anger "He snorted like a horse." He was grieved with the sorrow of Mary and Martha but there was anger in His soul at the agony that Satan has brought to mankind. Paul gloried in tribulation but he did not glorify tribulation. He called his thorn in the flesh "the messenger of Satan" and wrote that he was hindered from visiting the Thessalonians—not "Providentially detained" as we preachers sometimes say—but hindered by Satan. Jesus spoke of that poor woman "whom Satan hath bound."

There are innumerable "Whys?" about all the misery and torture of this old world. Our Lord was not a guru in some Shangri-La doling out wordy platitudes. He lived among us in the daily affairs of men, a woodworker until He was thirty, a preacher, teacher, healer; but above all else He was the Son of God. He did not explain the mystery of sin; He came not to brush away the cobwebs but to kill the spider! Did He groan about bringing Lazarus back to earth? Lazarus was one of the few who have died twice. He had been only a few hours in glory, just looking around maybe, and he was called to return. His presence brought to a high pitch the rising opposition to Jesus. We do not know what happened to him. Any man touched by Jesus Christ is good publicity for the Gospel. Do not grumble if some come to church out of curiosity—just as many came to Bethany to see Lazarus—they may see Jesus! He

61

is a poor Christian who does not weep and trouble his soul and, yes, even burn with anger at what Satan is doing to this poor world.

All His earthly life our Saviour was aware of His special mission—"mine hour" he called its climax in the Garden of Gethsemane when He said to His enemies "This is *your hour* and the power of darkness." His hour and their hour! There God and the devil met in head-on collision. The last scenes of that conflict have not yet appeared but in a victory already won, our Waterloo is behind us. Meanwhile we may weep as Jesus wept, but not as those who have no hope.

21

The Groaning Christian

"We that are in this tabernacle do groan," Paul said. There is nothing neurotic or morbid about being homesick for heaven. The tenant of this mortal body longs for his new body. Even death is sometimes welcome as the door to that transition. I have read of a poor fellow who was dreadfully seasick. A cheerful soul, such as always shows up at such times, said to the sufferer, "Cheer up, seasickness never killed anybody." "Don't tell me that," was the reply. "It's the hope of dying that has kept me alive this long!"

The hope of dying can become a welcome prospect to the suffering saint when it means exchanging groans for glory. Actually we human beings never really see the tenant within the tenement. I look into your eyes but I do not see the actual you, call it spirit, soul or what you will. Your eyes cannot see; you see with your eyes. Your ears do not hear; you hear with your ears. Your tongue cannot talk; you talk with your tongue. You can see a brain but not a mind. One day the little machine we call a body will go out of business and it is "ashes to ashes and dust to dust." What happens to the tenant when the tenement collapses? The spirit of the Christian goes to be with Christ. There is much we do not understand about what form of manifestation we assume between death and the resurrection. But the groaning will be past!

The Christian meets with sorrow, accidents, sickness and death. All the tribulations of this life are but incidents on the road from Groans to Glory, and a Christian is not a citizen of earth trying to get to heaven but a citizen of heaven making his way through this world.

This groaning of the Christian is not to be confused with griping and grumbling. If we growl all day we shouldn't be surprised if we end up dog tired at night! No, we are living in The Great Until and we are in the middle of the book of God's purpose—past, present and future. We see through a glass as in a riddle, an enigma. You cannot make a sensible estimate in the middle of the book. Fix your eyes on the glory to come and then what looks dark in the distance will brighten as you draw near. Remember, the road from Groans to Glory is by grace and there will always be enough of that to do all that God wants you to do as long as He wants you to do it.

22

The Groaning Comforter

We call Him the Comforter but He also groans for us. We know not what we should pray for as we ought so He prays for us with unutterable intercession. What all this means we cannot fully comprehend, but one thing is certain: if our condition is such and our need is so great that the Holy Spirit prays for us with unutterable groanings we had better do some groaning ourselves! When one beholds the casual faces of church-goers on Sunday mornings he wonders whether they ever knew this kind of concern, utterable or unutterable! Their fathers used to sing,

> Twas grace that taught my heart to fear,
> And grace my fears relieved;
> How precious did that grace appear
> The hour I first believed!

Nowadays sin is nothing to bother about, the Judgment Day is a joke, and having no godly fear we know no godly relief.

When we get the groan of holy concern into our praying according to God's Word, God's will, our need and our faith, we will not be disappointed. It cannot fail. Working out God's will in our lives is not always pleasant; conformity to the likeness of His Son involves obedience and discipline. The Holy Spirit knows what God wills in our lives and sometimes that means groaning, but it opens up one day into joy unspeakable and full of glory. Moreover as we go along we taste the powers of the age to come, the "foretaste of glory divine."

The hill of Zion yields
A thousand sacred sweets
Before we reach the heavenly fields,
Or walk the golden streets.

While we groan we also grow and "our light affliction, *which is but for a moment,*" is working out for us a far more exceeding "weight of glory." So the grace, the groans and the glory are all part of the eternal purpose. Where there is no groaning there is no growing now, nor glory to come. Thank God, the Divine Groaner is also the Comforter, the One-Called-Alongside-to-Help while we travel from Groans to Glory.

23

Lord of What's Left

My father should have been a preacher. He felt the call as a young man but the cares of daily life and making a living made preparation seem impossible. Two of his brothers became ministers, one a Baptist and the other a Methodist. All his days father was faithful in the little country church and a true Christian in the home community. But he always felt that he was trying to settle for second best and he was never filled with the joy of fulfillment.

In my own ministry I have faced many listeners who have heard the divine summons but never said "Yes." They may have succeeded to some extent in another field but were haunted all their lives with what Paul Laurence Dunbar, the black poet, put so well: "Nobody else can do the job that God's marked out for you." Some have heard God's call to Africa or China or some other distant field but willingness to go across the street will not suffice when God said, "Go across the sea."

I do not believe, however, that we can compensate by living the rest of our days in regret and self-condemnation. To waste the remainder of our days in penance for the call we missed does no good for God or man.

> What then? Shall we sit down and idly say,
> "The night hath come, it is no longer day"?
> The night hath not yet come, we are not quite
> Cut off from labour by the failing light;
> Something remains for us to do and dare.
> Even the oldest trees some fruit may bear
> For age is opportunity no less

> Than youth itself tho' in another dress.
> And as the evening twilight fades away
> The sky is filled with stars invisible by day.

Longfellow said it well. God will forgive the truly repentant heart. The new task may not be so great but the harvest is plenteous and the laborers are few. Too many are willing to sit at God's table but not to work in His fields! I have known some who got off to a late start but far outdid others who started young but lacked the prod that goes to lateness and missed the laziness that often goes with the young who boast, "There's plenty of time!"

There is still time to pray:

> Lord of the years that are left to me,
> I give them to Thy hand;
> Take me and make me and mould me
> To the pattern Thou hast planned.

Why not make him *Lord of What's Left!* What is left of my time, what is left of me, my strength, my abilities, all I am and have. As with the feeding of the multitude with loaves and fishes, what might not still be wrought with the pieces left over! Blessed are they who begin early in the vineyard—but better late than never. Bring the broken threads, the scraps and lay it all at His feet. He who restores the years "the locust hath eaten" may do a wonder with leftovers. At any rate, if you failed to crown Him early make Him *Lord of What's Left!*

24

The All-Inclusive Invitation

For many years of my ministry I closed my sermons with invitations to every category of people I could think of. I appealed to the unsaved, the unsure—those who were not sure of their salvation—the undedicated who had not yielded everything to Christ, the undecided as to their life work. As a result my listeners were often confused as to which bracket they belonged to or what they were coming forward to do.

One day it dawned upon me that Romans 10:9,10 did not cover only the unsaved but that confessing Jesus as Lord covers every possible classification. It assures certainty of salvation, "You shall be saved." Certainly, to confess Jesus as Lord means dedication of life, separation from the world, one's life work, everything. Let a man get right on the Lordship of Christ and he is right all down the line on every issue. It means that the flagship of the fleet is the Lordship of Christ and if that ship leads, all the other ships—church membership, fellowship, discipleship, stewardship, worship—will follow the flagship!

Jesus Christ demands confession with the mouth before men—audible, visible and credible (believing with the heart). It is more than saying "Jesus is Lord" ... He *is* Lord whether we ever confess Him or not, for one day every knee shall bow and every tongue confess His Lordship. But I must confess Him as *my* Lord if I am to be a saved, sure, surrendered, separated servant of His.

So now I call upon everybody not merely to walk down a church aisle and shake hands with the preacher while the choir sings, "Have Thine Own Way, Lord." I ask them to stand and say aloud, "I confess Jesus (which means 'Saviour') as *my* Lord." Of course, we can say it and not mean it ("why call ye me, Lord, Lord, and do not the things which I say?"). Jesus declared that at the judgment some would say, "We have prophesied, done mighty works, cast out demons" only to hear Him say, "Depart from me, you workers of iniquity." We must mean what we say, from the heart man "believeth unto salvation." I believe this one-shot invitation wraps it all up whatever classification one belongs to. People will not be doing a dozen different things; they will be doing one thing, confessing Jesus as Lord and, doing that, they will be getting saved, sure, dedicated, separated from the world, as the need may be. Even growing Christians will be reaffirming their faith, which is a good thing to do . . . you do not tell your wife just once for all that you love her!

I believe this is what the early Christians did and it took care of everything. If we make clear what the Lordship of Christ really means the issue is simplified and people know what they are doing. It is an initial affirmation when we become Christians. It is a continuous affirmation the rest of our days.

In the Roman Empire, every one was required to put a pinch of incense on the altar and confess Caesar as Lord. Christians would not do this and many died for their faith. Some who carved images for the public, although not worshiping the images themselves, tried to excuse themselves by saying, "I have to make a living and this is how I do it." Tertullian, mighty Christian of his day, would reply, "Must you live?" They had and we have but one Lord and we do not have to live; we have only to be true to Jesus Christ, live or die, come what may. If Jesus is Lord, that ends it. We count not our lives dear even unto death, not merely until death. Jesus is Lord.

Peter said once, "Not so, Lord." But if we say, "Not so," He is not Lord, and if He is Lord we do not say, "Not so"!

25

"Like a Motherless Child"

"Sometimes I feel like a motherless child." So says the old spiritual and so say many of us who walk the valley of loneliness. Never have we had so much amusement and entertainment and never so many who walk alone. Even youth with every device to make life interesting sets a record in suicide. It does not help to be in a big crowd—who is ever lonelier than a stranger in a city! And the social set that dines and dances and frolics the night away sits "after the ball is over" drugged and dismal. Like Job in his distress they ask, "When shall I arise, and the night be gone?"

The Saviour's disciples faced His cross and His departure. They had walked the roads of Galilee with the Son of God. Life would never be the same again. They had been with Jesus Christ for three years and they could not go back. They had experienced a foretaste of glory and now He was going away. He sought to prepare them to make it through this world the rest of their days when they would no longer see Him. What He said prepares us also who have never seen Him and yet, twenty centuries later, have believed in order that we may walk these roads of earth until "the day break and the shadows flee away."

Our Lord would return to His disciples for a brief forty days. He will come for us. Meanwhile there will be days when we feel like a motherless child. But He said, "I will not leave you comfortless." "I will not leave you *orphans*"! He promised to be with us *all the days* and the Holy Spirit is the One who walks alongside to help. Where two or three gather in His

71

Name you will find Jesus. It is not just a promise but a fact and in the hours when we are least aware of Him we can carry on, feel like it or not, until the light breaks through.

I remember a night in my meetings when a choral group from a children's home sang for us. These little tykes knew nothing of their fathers or mothers but they sang,

> From the door of an orphanage to the house of a King,
> No longer an outcast, a new song I sing.
> From rags unto riches, from the weak to the strong,
> I'm not worthy to be here but, praise God, I belong!

I sat there and listened with a lump in my throat as big as an apple!

"When my father and my mother forsake me, then the Lord will take me up." If we have put our trust in Jesus we belong to the family of God in heaven and on earth. No orphans there! For He said that if we follow Him we shall gain fathers and mothers, sisters and brothers, and in that new fellowship everybody is kinfolks!

No place to feel like a motherless child!

26

Have We Misread Our Script?

Some years ago there was considerable interest in tracing roots of all kinds—ethnic, family, religious. Ancestry is a fascinating study but the best part, as with potatoes, is usually under the ground. Investigating the family tree is risky business and can be embarrassing.

The roots of our Christian faith begin with a humble virgin mother and babe in a cattle stall in Bethlehem. Maybe some professed Christians are ashamed of the Gospel because its beginnings are hard on fleshly pride. If we had set up the advent of God's Son we certainly never would have started with such a lowly birth. I have always been struck with the way Luke paints the sharp contrast of Caesar Augustus and worldwide taxation and, against that impressive background, a peasant couple headed for Bethlehem with no room reservations for the greatest birth in history. We would have had our Lord come to earth full-grown, a world traveler, university lecturer. Think what the news media could have done for Him! Instead, when He performed a miracle, He said, "Don't tell it!" His brothers urged Him to get out of the backwoods and up on the boulevards. He needed a good press agent! He did miracles and never advertised them. Today we advertise them but cannot do them!

And when He chose twelve disciples, why didn't He convert a dozen scholarly rabbis to be the spearhead of His movement? Instead He picked a miscellaneous band of fishermen, tax collectors and other nonentities, rookies nobody would have looked at a second time. Later on Saul of Tarsus was added, an alumnus of the school of Gamaliel but he counted all that but loss, writing that not many wise, mighty and noble are called, and dedicated himself to the "foolishness of preaching."

When Jesus rose from the dead, why didn't He appear before Herod, Caiaphas and Pilate? He had the greatest news break of all time. Instead He says "Mary" to a weeping woman, breaks bread in an Emmaus home, and tells disciples how to catch fish after a night of failure! Such simple things do not seem to fit into those precious forty days. We would have tried to get the word all over the Roman Empire. MAN WHO CLAIMS TO BE THE SON OF GOD COMES BACK FROM THE GRAVE!

God never planned or promised that true Christians would ever be anything more than a persecuted minority, scorning the values of this world and living under rigid discipline, swimming against the stream of this world's thinking and living. As long as they followed that pattern they turned the world upside down. Later, Constantine became a church member and made it fashionable to be a professed Christian. We have never fully recovered from that awful blunder. Now and then a new company gets back to roots, and revival restores something of that primitive glory of the early church. What the world needs is neither a Christless churchianity nor a churchless Christianity, but Christ the Head living afresh in His body, the Church.

In our zeal to make the Gospel acceptable, fashionable—we have put the ark on a Philistine cart instead of carrying it on dedicated shoulders. We thought to speed it up by putting it on modern wheels, but we actually stop the procession, as happened with David, and we suffer tragedy as did Uzzah. It is time to return to our roots and begin at the beginning. The gait of Galilee and the pattern of Pentecost call for fresh study.

Have we misread our script today?

27

Don't Push the Plow

In the rural community where I grew up many a small farmer plowed with a mule. That was no easy life. A mule is a problem to begin with and trying to steer a plow through that red dirt and roots and rocks tested any son of the soil. I always felt that it required an extra supply of grace to be a farmer in those days with a few acres, a primitive plow and a stubborn mule.

Our Saviour gave us a solemn word about putting one's hand to the plow and looking back. There are other angles of this business that carry lessons for Christians. For one thing, we make the mistake of "pushing the plow." The farmer had to keep his plow in the furrow and guide its course but it was the mule's business to pull the plow. A lot of energy can be spent trying to push what can only be pulled. Let the mule bear the responsibility of pulling the plow. Our business as Christians is to make a straight course and keep the plow in the furrow, but the power to pull the plow through to the finish is God's, not ours. We work ourselves up in the energy of the flesh trying to do God's part of the work. He works in us to will and to do. Our part is to keep a straight furrow and the plow on its course.

Some other farm proverbs come to mind. Did you ever hear of drowning in a mud puddle? It is possible to be submerged and overcome by trivial matters not that important. It is no disgrace to be the victim of a lion but there is no excuse for allowing ourselves to be bitten to death by mosquitoes. Many a dear soul allows the minor vexations and petty nuisances of life to defeat him when he should have been absorbed with matters of greater worth. We drown in mud puddles of insignificant issues and have no time for great concerns. We need to seek first the kingdom of God and His righteousness and not let what we eat and wear and all life's lesser interests take up our time. They will be added, our Lord said, but we should let God add them while we are busy with His Word and will and work.

I have heard also of "wearing a sailor suit to cross a creek." We give too much importance to lesser matters, make a big show out of small performances, burn up a gallon of energy on a pint-size project. We dress up mint, anise and cumin and neglect judgment, mercy and faith. Now one must wear some sort of outfit even to cross a creek, but don't make a Rubicon out of it. It is like working up a mass parade and staging fireworks just to campaign for dogcatcher.

We tend to magnify the minor and minimize the major. A lot of religious activity today burns up time and money on phylacteries and long prayers and seats in the synagogue and straining at gnats while we swallow camels, and the great issues get lost in all the fanfare about nonessentials.

Let the mule pull the plow. Don't drown in a mud puddle. Don't put on an admiral's uniform to get across a lake. Trimming things to their right size and importance would be the best conservation measure I know.

28

Waiting for the Postman

Since I am away from my base most of the time my mail is my lifeline. My sister-in-law lives nearby down the next street. She takes care of my mail and forwards some of it when necessary. Sometimes letters get to my own box and accumulate. The system breaks down once in a while and I can't help turning time backward in its flight and in memory I revert to my boyhood days in the country when we had only one postman (we called him the "mail carrier") all the years from my boyhood to young manhood. The same man served all those years from horse-and-buggy and dirt road days to automobiles and highways.

My postman was a likable, jolly man who was never in a hurry, often chatting with my father on his route. He liked to sing and many a day I could hear him coming up "The Cut" to the top of the hill where we lived, singing at the top of his strong voice either some hymn or maybe a popular song like "When I Grow Too Old to Dream I'll Have You to Remember." There was not a lot of mail but along with the letters (three-cent stamps!) we had the *Literary Digest* in those days, the *Time* and *Newsweek* and *U.S. News* of that era.

I remember 1912 when the *Titanic* went down. I was eleven but the shock remains. It was the first in a series that might be called "The Sinking of the Unsinkable," an object lesson we failed to learn. Then came 1914 and World War I which we thought just couldn't happen. Life would never be the same again. The same postman served our route until the good years of the century gave way to the "delirium tremens" of the mod-

ern madhouse. Today in the weird insanity of these times mis-
named "Progress" I have now and then a spell of wishing I
could sit once more as a boy on the old porch of that old house
(still standing, believe it or not!) and hear Postman Johnson
coming up The Cut singing "When I Grow Too Old to
Dream."

Don't start your arguments for these times. I know them and
agree with some of them. This is no plea for a return to "the
good old days" that weren't so good sometimes—the age of
kerosene lamps, dirt roads, horse-and-buggy travel. But I do
have an unhappy suspicion that somewhere in the Great Transition we threw the baby out with the bathwater. I'm too old
and tired to fuss about it. Strangely enough I have reached
eighty in the busiest and most fruitful years of a long, long
ministry since 1913. God has been so good to me that I'm not
bemoaning the passing of better days. But the overall picture
of this epoch is a different story. I listen to the experts pool
their ignorance in symposiums and team up on TV trying to
analyze the whats and whys of this weird mess that has become
a madhouse instead of a millennium.

And I'd still like to sit a spell on the old porch back home
and listen with memory's ears to the postman coming up The
Cut singing "When I Grow Too Old to Dream I'll Have You to
Remember."

29

Smart But Not Safe

I was away from home when the astronauts made one of their voyages to the moon. In a motel room as I watched them on television I could look out the window into a park. It was safe for the astronauts to walk on the moon, but I dared not take a walk in that park—I might be clobbered, robbed, even killed. I thought: *smart enough to walk on the moon—not safe enough to walk in the park!* Such is the paradox of Progress. The prime delusion of history is the notion that man without God will create eventually, by his sophisticated know-how, heaven on earth. The Parthenon, the Colosseum, the Caesars and Charlemagnes, the Hitlers and Mussolinis, all testify that they belonged to the losing side. Nuclear wonders, DNA and test-tube babies feed our pride and modern man feels no need of God. We think that Humanism can work out its own salvation, and not with fear and trembling but in boastful self-worship. One of these days our Tower of Babel will be incinerated by the awesome power we have discovered but cannot control.

Civilization is doomed, for the Old Adam cannot control his own devices. God sent His Son to earth to call out a people for His Name. That race, the twice-born, will never be accepted by this world. They are sheep among wolves as their Saviour said. They will never control the culture of their day but one day Jesus Christ will return and will reign with His people on a redeemed earth. Paul Harvey said that Christians believe Jesus Christ will return and take over when mortals have made a hopeless mess of self-government. Then He could be back any day! We have just about done it! The Christian cause is the

only one that is bound to win. It may seem to fail but it is better to fail now and then in a cause that will one day succeed
than succeed in a cause that will one day fail. We are part of an
incoming tide. Our little waves may be defeated but the tide is
sure to win!

The leader of that Cause seemed to fail when he hung between two thieves and cried, "My God, my God, why hast
thou forsaken me?" It looked like Herod and Pilate had won.
But then Christ rose from the dead and He leads a procession
of saints who may not look like it but are the ultimate winners
in the final showdown. Of course they try to improve conditions and make things better wherever possible, but they are
not looking for a pagan world to lift itself up by its own boot-
straps. They are gathering others, comrades to take over when
unregenerate men go down in utter defeat. "The meek shall inherit the earth." Others may have a lease but the meek hold the
deed!

Such a world view irks the wise, the mighty and the noble
but not many of them have been chosen. This present culture
looks down with disdain on that band of exiles and aliens who
are looking for the Great White City that's soon coming down.
We pilgrims and strangers are not much impressed by all the
expertise of the natural man. Our message is "moronic" to him,
foolishness to the world and we are to the world fools. But this
age became a generation of fools professing themselves to be
wise. No use telling them what they are for the god of this age
has blinded their minds. Their only hope is in being born again
and getting their eyes opened just as was the case with that
Pharisee of the Pharisees who started out with orders and credentials from the organized religion of his day to put the
church out of business. On the Damascus Road he met Jesus
Christ and was blinded by the glory of that light, but his eyes
were opened—blinded forever to the charms of this world, but
opened forever to another world. And he who started out to
put the church out of business spent the rest of his days putting
churches in business!

30

Thoughts at Random

With my usual proclivity for crossing bridges before I reach them I dreaded changing planes in the huge new terminal. I saw myself out of breath rushing pell-mell to the gate of my next flight which of course would be at the other end of the place. All set for that sprint I found it to be only four doors down the hall and myself with oodles of time to spare! I grinned sheepishly and asked myself, "When will you ever learn!"

All these years the preceding angel has gone ahead while I wondered who would roll away the stone from the sepulcher. I am glad my Father knows my frame and remembers that I am dust. The smoking flax He will not quench and the bruised reed He will not break. Like Mr. Fearing in *Pilgrim's Progress* I have often wondered how it will be when I finally get home. I dare to believe that it will be infinitely brighter than I have sometimes dared to hope. "When I tread the verge of Jordan, bid my anxious fears subside!" I dare think that He who fed the worried prophet in his lowest mood under the juniper, He who did not rebuke John the Baptist languishing in jail, He who asked the disciple who had denied Him, "Lovest thou me?" when he had boasted he would never fail . . . will He not be strongest when we are weakest and welcome us when we scarcely lift up our eyes? As with Mr. Fearing, I ask—may Jordan be lowest at my crossing time and may I make it "not much above wet-shod!"

Can I doubt His tender mercy who through life has been my Guide? Will not the God of the Hitherto be the God of the

Henceforth? Through many dangers, toils and snares I have already come, and will not the grace that brought me safe thus far be sure to lead me home?

"Yet is their strength labour and sorrow" even if we make it to fourscore. I am eighty now. Teach me to number my days that I may apply my heart unto wisdom. May the last chapter be the best, may I finish my course with joy. Give me, like the tribe of Issachar, understanding of the times, to know what Israel, God's people, ought to do. Not mere knowledge but understanding and wisdom, which is just about the scarcest commodity these days. We know many things today but wisdom is the proper use of knowledge. The problems today are beyond the politicians, the sophisticates, the experts. We do not know WHAT these days, much less HOW! The issue is WHOM to know and when we know Him we know WHAT and HOW. He is made unto us wisdom. Paul asked, "WHO art Thou?" before "WHAT wilt Thou have me to do?"

Grant me in these pressurized times to walk much alone, not too closely identified with any individual, group or movement, with time to tramp the woods, to linger long in quiet spots, and listen to the wood thrush chime his vespers. Spare me the fate of Rip Van Winkle who slept through a revolution and woke up hollering for the wrong George! Keep me from telling too much to anybody and help me to keep my cool and spill everything only to God. Let me not major on any spoke but stay at the hub of God's truth and not end up out on the rim! By Jesus Christ all things consist and we are complete in Him. If we stand at the Hub all the spokes are ours! For all the spokes are His and all things are ours—except ourselves. We are His and He is God's!

31

There's Always Light in Goshen!

When Jacob brought all his family to Egypt at the invitation of Joseph, they settled in Egypt in "the country of Goshen." Today God's people, the Church, of the kingdom of heaven, live in Egypt, as it were, in this world but not of it. They are a spiritual colony of heaven. Not citizens of earth going to heaven, but citizens of heaven making their way through this world, pilgrims and strangers, exiles and aliens, a holy nation within the nation, the family of God.

For a while the children of Jacob lived in peace but there arose a king "who knew not Joseph" and the Israelites became slaves in Egypt. Then God raised up Moses who said, "Let my people go." But when Pharaoh said "No," the plagues began to fall. We read that when the plague of darkness fell the Egyptians could not even see each other but "the children of Israel had light in their dwellings." *When it was dark in Egypt it was light in Goshen!*

Today God's people live in this world, subject to all the accidents, the diseases, the disasters and troubles that beset all men. In this world we have tribulation but we are children of the kingdom of day and we are not stumbling in the darkness. We live in an unseen world amidst a visible creation, we walk in the Light as He is in the light, we have meat to eat of which this world knows nothing. We look not at the seen but at the unseen, not at the temporal but at the eternal. Christians live in the same world with everybody else, subject to the same natural laws of cause and effect, often beset by the same infirmities, tried and afflicted. But we are the Children of the Day, not of the Darkness. We believe in a God who is greater than all His laws, who transcends them in ways not contranatural but supernatural. We may sometimes be hard hit by cause and effect, when Satan's darts at us are hurled. But having first come to Jesus, we become and we overcome, even as we live visibly in Egypt while our hearts reside in Goshen. Our lives are hid with Christ in God; we are "homed" in God, and whatever happens, we cannot die away from home! Though now we see Him not, *yet believing,* we rejoice with joy unspeakable and full of glory. And, no matter how dark it is in Egypt, there is always light in Goshen!

The earthquake, the hurricane, the flood may break, as it did in Toccoa, Georgia, drowning thirty-nine of that Christian community. But it will be said of the survivors as it was reported of the saints in Toccoa, "They didn't crack up and panic; they had something else!" The doctor may say, "It is cancer," and all earthly hope may fade, but while the body agonizes in Egypt the soul abides in Goshen.

And when the New Jerusalem comes down and we dwell in the City of God, we read "there shall be no night there." I have never been fond of night and darkness. I rise at an unearthly hour to see the night depart and usher in the day. I watch for the dawn and long for that bright and cloudless morning when the dead in Christ shall rise. Until then I live in the Egypt of this old world but my soul dwells in Goshen. And no matter how dark it gets in Egypt God's people have light in their dwellings even as long ago.

32

Maggie Valley

I sit in my motel room in Maggie Valley, deep in the Carolina mountains. It is late afternoon and my window opens on a lovely little church surrounded by the glory of springtime in May and behind it rises the majesty of the Blue Ridge peaks sturdy and serene. I am a tired preacher after weeks on the road and this season is balm to my soul.

I like the name "Maggie Valley." It has a "mountainy" ring like the hillbilly ballads of this mountain country. It speaks of a way of life now almost gone, hounded out by the march of "Progress"—highways and real estaters and developments now gobbling up what is left of this gentle age when there was time to live, to be still, to watch the sun go down, to hear the whippoorwill and the 'possum hunters at night. One remembers the family that sat around the fire discussing an absent relative who was getting rich promoting the new age. When someone observed, "I hear he is getting on in the world," grandmother asked from her chair in the corner, "Which world?"

I hear that the new superhighway has bypassed Maggie Valley. The New Day has already passed it which is no reflection on Maggie Valley. A lot of Maggie Valleys are being bypassed these days by the new thoroughfares of these times, just as we whiz along with eyes glued to the road and blind to the beauty we have no time to see. In the delirium around us no matter how much time we save and how soon we can get from Dan to Beersheba, we have lost more than we have gained, growing richer in what money can buy and poorer in what it cannot buy.

Maggie Valley speaks volumes to those who can sit at the end of a perfect day like this and engage in the lost art of meditation. Most of the breakneck speedsters will only smile at a lonely preacher watching a sundown in Maggie Valley. No use explaining it to them. Years of living as we do today has immunized most of us from what I am writing about. Here and there some kindred soul will understand and a weary face will light up when faint reminders of the life that was touch the strings of memory.

The world of things spiritual is going through something similar to Maggie Valley. A modern hymnal no longer contains the dear old favorite "Take Time To Be Holy." It takes time to be holy and we don't have time! Happy is that soul that rekindles the fire of a simpler faith, refuses to sell out to the promoters of Progress, and still seeks the old paths to find rest within.

Today this drugged, drunk, doped generation pitifully tries to induce chemically a tranquillity that does not come that way. Peace is not packaged in pills.

The Son of God who brought peace to earth spent much time on the mountain or by the sea. He rose a great while before day to seek a solitary place and pray. He said to His disciples, "Come ye yourselves apart and rest awhile." I wrote it long ago in one of my books, "If you don't come apart you *will* come apart!" I believe that I have been helped much these fourscore years by having found Maggie Valleys along my pilgrimage.

33

"Is Not This the Carpenter?"

I cannot remember ever having heard a sermon on the Hidden Years at Nazareth. With a whole world to save, our Lord waited until He was thirty to begin His public ministry. And when He did teach in the Nazareth synagogue His listeners could not rise above the fact that He was one of the local boys and so, as He Himself said, the prophet was without honor in His own country.

Why did the Son of God spend all those years in a woodworker's shop? Why did He not visit Rome and Athens and Alexandria and lecture in the great world centers? And why did He spend by far the greater portion of His earthly life as a carpenter! It does not add up on our little computers in this publicity-mad era of the mass media when people will do anything under the sun to land on the front page and show up on television.

Whatever other reasons He may have had, I am persuaded that my Saviour made Himself of no reputation and followed this lowly trade with hammer and saw to make it clear that the life He came to bring and live—and which He Himself *was* and *is*—can be lived out in this humdrum world of the ordinary day-by-day experiences of men. The Christ life is not reserved for cloistered saints in secluded retreats, revelling in ecstasies and mystic meditation. Christ lives again in hearts that believe and receive Him. He lives still in carpenters and truck drivers and farmers and factory workers as well as doctors, lawyers, executives, teachers and artists, and in kitchens where godly housewives and mothers have not surrendered to the "new-woman" mania. If it cannot be lived in the shop, there is no sense in preaching it in the sanctuary!

Right here is a serious problem today. We are an emotionally drunken generation, not sophisticated but sick, trying to live on trances and vibrations and trips to a third heaven and looking with (un)holy disdain on ordinary Christians on the old Straight-and-Narrow, Trust-and-Obey Road to heaven.

I am glad that my Lord was a carpenter and not a celebrity for thirty years. That makes Him one of us ordinary mortals, touched with a feeling of our infirmities, tempted in all points like as we and yet without sin. His life is best proven Monday through Saturday out where cross the crowded ways of men, and not in church conventions and occasional religious extravaganzas.

The greatest of all Gospel preachers, the Apostle Paul, was not a carpenter but a tentmaker and that is not any higher up the totem pole. The rich, the wise, the mighty and noble can be saved, though not many are called; but the main bulk of the church are saints in the lower brackets. The common people heard Him gladly and most of His best listeners still are found in that category.

I am glad the Son of God was a carpenter and not an ascetic in the wilderness, or a scholarly scribe in the temple. The Nazarenes may still say, "How knoweth this man (wisdom) having never learned?" but the genesis and genius of what we call Christianity started in a Bethlehem manger and at a Nazareth woodworker's bench. The whole story is still foolishness to the world that crucified Him but while they scorned Him and still do they could not and cannot stop Him even though they killed Him and buried Him in a sealed tomb. He came out and He will come back, not seated on a carpenter's bench but on a Conqueror's throne.

34

Chattanooga Choo-Choo

I had Sunday dinner at the Chattanooga Choo-Choo where enterprising citizens of that lovely city have turned the old rail-road terminal station into a marvelous complex of restaurants, fountains, terraces and restored trains with sleepers. If you want to turn time backward and sleep in a Pullman one more time you can do it there. The visit kindled my nostalgia and carried me back to the days when I rode home many a time on the Carolina Special or when Sara and I took off at night on the Crescent for California. "Precious memories, how they linger!" A blessed retreat for a few dear moments into yesterday, and yesteryear.

Nobody wants to return to dirt roads, kerosene lamps, horse-and-buggy travel. But somewhere along the many-laned highways of today we have grown richer in the things money can buy and poorer in the things we can't buy. We have gained a new world and lost our souls.

Someone commented on one of our past World Fairs, "The theme of the Fair was the achievements of science and their application through industry to the creation of a larger life for all mankind. We could see the achievements of science and their application through industry but we looked in vain for the larger life for all mankind."

A *longer* life for some, perhaps. But so what? Life is not measured by length but by depth. Birthdays tell how long we have been on the road, not how far we have traveled. We now have a record host of old folks like me, some of them saying,

I can see with my bifocals;
My dentures work just fine;
I can live with my arthritis,
But I sure do miss my mind!

Retirement homes are filled with the aged, just waiting to die, in this new prolongation of death, not life.

Not a *finer* life either. Two centuries of ancient Athens produced men who set standards in statesmanship, philosophy, letters, oratory and art for all subsequent time. We mistake being informed for being wise. "If you need knowledge, go to school. If you need wisdom, get on your knees!"

History's biggest joke is the delusion called Progress. The Tower of Babel is repeated in every generation through the centuries. Mankind will not reach heaven by its own devices. It will end in catastrophe, in the shattered wreckage of its own inventions. We are trying to play the ball game without the ball.

I ride a jet every few days now; then I rush from panicky airport to crowded motel. And millions of mortals crowd highways trying to get away from it all. But we don't enjoy vacations because we have to take ourselves along. An hour or two at the Chattanooga Choo-Choo is a blessed respite. It takes you back to when we had time. Nowadays we don't have time to go in thirty minutes where we once could go . . . and take all day.

I'd like one more ride on the Carolina Special. And I feel like humming, "When that midnight choo-choo leaves for Alabam'." ALL ABOARD!

35

The Step and the Walk

A recent letter from a couple, two dear friends who attended my meetings, closed with this comment, "We love you because you led us from the step to the walk." Much is said about the step of faith when one receives Jesus Christ as Saviour or makes a vow of dedication, a new start in Christian living. But we are told in Colossians 2:6, "As ye have therefore received Christ Jesus the Lord, *so walk ye in him.*" The step must become a walk, a succession of steps day by day as we walk in the light, walk in love, walk as Jesus walked. Our churches are filled with people who have never moved from the step to the walk. After conversion comes continuance. After our Lord invites us to come to Him and receive His rest He immediately tells us to take His yoke upon us, learn of Him and find rest. Rest is both an obtainment and an attainment and too many believers matriculate but never go to school.

Some are habitual "steppers," constantly getting converted, making new decisions, forming fresh resolves; but they never go on toward perfection. They are always seeking some new experience and bounding from one mountaintop to another but they never travel the valleys between in discipline. The step never becomes the walk.

Such "steppers" enjoy the excitement of new decisions but they are poor travelers on the daily pilgrimage. The Christian life has its long stretches of hard work and sometimes it seems drudgery when the initial glow fades and the slow grind tries the soul. Some faithful plodders irritate these excitable souls who start out with a bang and soon end in a bog. Such exhortations as, "Let us go on," "Let us run the race," are for these great beginners who never finish what they begin.

My admiration is reserved for those steady saints who may not shout during the revival but who keep walking the old Straight and Narrow long after those who followed the step with a stop have fallen by the wayside. Our Lord worked at a carpenter's bench until He was thirty to make plain that the life He came to give can and must be lived out over the long and sometimes humdrum stretch and is not a matter of fits and starts.

An occasional reaffirmation of our faith and dedication is a good thing to bring us up to date, but it is no substitute for patient continuance. Revivals bring great blessing but a host of new recruits that never go to battle is no real gain for the Church. We are in desperate need of bringing a host of church members from the step to the walk. Beginning to build without finishing brought reproof from our Lord who in his illustrations of the man building a tower and the king going to war emphasized "sitting down first" to count the cost and make a study of the issues involved. Beginning the Christian life or making a fresh dedication is not a matter of snap judgment and superficial enthusiasm. God wants us to mean what we are doing. The way is straight and narrow and few there are who find it. It begins with a step but from there on we keep stepping as we practice what we profess in the home, at work, in whatever we do, doing all to the glory of God.

It is a great day for Christians and churches when the step becomes a walk!

36

The Turn of the Tide

Years ago I saw somewhere the line, "The lowest ebb is the turn of the tide," and it has lingered with me. The waves on the beach advance and recede and when they have retreated to the farthest point, it will not be long until the advance begins. You can set your watch by it. The lowest ebb marks the turn of the tide.

There have been in my own experience three times of low ebb and high tide. I have already written of one of them back in the late twenties and early thirties when my doctrine was weakest and then voice and vision returned and I began to preach afresh the old message of my boyhood days.

The second low ebb was in 1940 when I left my church and began a traveling ministry. I have related in *Threescore and Ten* how I was suffering from nervous exhaustion and insomnia and yet felt called to start sleeping in a different bed each week, constantly readjusting to changing food, climate, environment. I headed for my first appointment in Grand Rapids, came down with the flu in Chicago and had to cancel my meetings. It was the lowest tide ever. I accepted an invitation to preach in Florida which I had previously declined and there I met the charming young lady who was willing later to share her life with a half-sick preacher who had little money and was not sure he could do what he had embarked upon as his life work. God's tide had come in at my lowest ebb! Sara Allred and I started out together and traveled all over the country for thirty-three years.

In 1973 she went to heaven and my ebb sank to a frightening

low. But God enabled me to write *Though I Walk Through The Valley* and the response was beyond all expectations. There was a new dimension in my experience and a new note in my preaching. Daybreak followed the darkest hour.

"There is a tide in the affairs of men," and history records many wanings and waxings. The ebb was low when Columbus discovered a new world. The Gates of Hercules marked the stop sign—"No More Beyond!" But for Columbus the "Stop" sign was a "Go" sign! John Wesley came along at low ebb. The Puritans had been buried and the Methodists had not been born!

The darkest low ebb was when our Saviour cried from the cross, "My God, my God, why hast thou forsaken me?" Then came the Crimson Tide of Calvary!

Waiting for God's tide to come is not sitting around like Mr. Micawber waiting for something to turn up. Nothing is more certain. But sometimes we do have to wait. Blessed is the man who becomes part of God's purpose. He will be on time in God's calendar by God's clock.

> O changeless sea, thy message
> In changing spray is cast.
> Within God's plan of progress
> It matters not at last
> How wide the shores of evil,
> how strong the reefs of sin,
> The wave may be defeated but the tide is sure to win!

What happens to your little wave is incidental but God's tide is sure to prevail. And it is better to fail in your highest expectations in a cause bound to succeed than to succeed in a cause doomed to fail.

37

"Among Those Present"

> I ask no dream, no prophet ecstasies,
> No sudden rending of the veil of clay,
> No angel visitant, no opening skies;
> But take the dimness of my soul away.

So wrote George Croly in that precious hymn, "Spirit of God, Descend Upon My Heart." And so say some of us who can report no revelations, no trip to third heaven. There was a time in my life when I sought those extra experiences of certain Christians about which I had read much. I sat up late and sought favored spots but to no avail. My temperament does not seem geared for such angel visitations. I remember sitting long ago deep in the woods on a lovely morning sure that this set-up would assure the "prophet ecstasy" I sought. I don't know when I have spent a duller morning utterly devoid of anything approaching a vision. A black crow perched in a tree just over me and cawed all morning as he eyed this intruder into the solitude. Instead of an angel there came a crow! Is it not often so?

I would not dispute the rare experiences some saints relate. I do think that sometimes their accounts grow and add new features as time goes on. If the story goes over, one is tempted to add details not in the original script. I suppose I am just plain vanilla and do not belong in the exotic fancy creams department.

I have no stock of amazing testimonies to relate. It is strange that an experience of miraculous healing brings down the house while a lifetime of good health by the grace of God brings only a yawn. Paul learned that far more important than a trip to Paradise or deliverance from a thorn in the flesh is to be able to prove the sufficiency of God's grace in strength through weakness. A daily walk with God rates higher on His scales than an occasional mountaintop thrill.

As life goes on, I rejoice that I do not *understand* but rather *know* that all things work together for good to me. I do not have to understand to know. I do not need to understand the process of digestion to know the pleasure of a good meal. I do not understand how television works but I know that it does and I can enjoy a good program—if I can find it! I do not understand how a mighty jet can carry its load across the sky but it does and I commit myself to it. I do not understand the process of God's purpose but I know it works for the people of that purpose.

I have seen religious movements and fads and vagaries come and go. I have seen stars and celebrities of "the deeper life" and "the higher life" and "the fuller life" make the rest of us yokels look like failures in our earthly pilgrimage. But we have made it through many dangers, toils and snares anyway, confident that grace will lead us home.

When the saints go marching home not all of them will have a chest full of medals. The best known soldier in Arlington National Cemetery is the Unknown Soldier! And it may be that when the redeemed throng finally assembles, more recognition than ever was accorded here will go to the host of good and faithful servants "among those present" who made it on the old T and O, Trust and Obey.

38

There's Always Mama

When I was a young preacher I used to bear down unmerci-fully on the saints in my congregation for being so quiet about their faith. I exhorted the redeemed of the Lord to say so, waxed vehement about being silent in an evil time and stormed about the importance of a faith that talks. I preached a vocal Christianity that confesses *with the mouth* Jesus as Lord. We al-ways had some who overdid saying so, who talked more reli-gion than they walked. There were long prayers and testi-monies that used up the time and let the meeting be run by a few loquacious souls. Strangely enough, come to think of it now, some of the best saints said least and never stole the show at prayer meeting.

I still believe we ought to talk about Jesus. The old country doctor of my boyhood days always began his examination by saying, "Let me see your tongue." That is a good way to check a Christian—the tongue test and what he is talking about. But the years have passed and my rules for separating the sheep from the goats are not so rigid on some points, notably the talk test. The reason is, I remember Mother.

Mama was one of the best Christians I ever knew. She was timid and shy and let Dad do most of the talking at home and abroad. She could sit in the old-time revivals in the little coun-try church when we had a shouting time and everybody got happy but she didn't join in. She believed in it and enjoyed it but it just wasn't her way.

I never heard her pray aloud. But she prayed. In the last year of her life one of the grandchildren slept near her. She says that on many a night when everybody was supposed to be asleep she could hear Mama whispering a prayer.

I know Mama was a Christian. I agree with whoever said:

> I have spent a lifetime seeking things I've spurned
>   when I have found them;
> I have fought and been rewarded in many a petty cause;
> But I'd give them all, fame, fortune and the pleasures
>   that go with them
> For a little of the faith
>   that made my mother what she was.

We are not all made alike and we do not well when we measure them all by our favorite yardstick. At the last Great Day there will be a big shake-up and a big shake-down. Servants who rode on horses and princes who walked will change places. True greatness in the sight of God will change our little picture of who's who.

I still wax eloquent on sinful silence and I like to see it broken. But lest I condemn some whom God has not condemned there creeps into memory one exception. I always think of Mama.

39

Like Him in This World

"As he is, so are we in this world" (1 John 4:17). Of all the New Testament writers John states the greatest truths in simplest terms. He clothes profundity with simplicity. Our text is a good sample. Can you say it in shorter words? Can you say a greater truth in *any* words!

There are many interpretations and applications of this text. It deals with love and judgment and identification with Christ. If He abides in us and we in Him, we need not be afraid or ashamed at the great judgment day. Perfect love casts out fear. Christ will never come into judgment and neither will we. The applications of the text stretch out in all directions but I want to look at it in its simplest form, just as it stands: "As he is, so are we in this world."

These nine little words fall into three sets of three words each. As He is—so are we—*in this world.*

"As He is." Not *as He was.* Between the eternity of a yesterday that never had a beginning and the eternity of a tomorrow that never will end, stands Jesus Christ the same. There is only one thing that Jesus Christ ever *was;* He was dead. "I am he that liveth *and was dead"* . . . but He is not dead now! He didn't stay dead. After the crucifixion Pilate and Herod and Caiaphas might have rubbed their hands and said, "That takes care of Him," but it didn't. They rolled a stone before that sepulcher, set a guard of soldiers and attached a seal but they did not take into consideration a mighty angel. Stones and soldiers and seals are no match for mighty angels. That angel rolled the stone away and sat on it as if to say, "Now look who's in charge around here!"

Jesus said: "I am he that liveth, and was dead; and, behold, I am alive for evermore." He said, "Before Abraham was, I am." John had seen Jesus in the days of His flesh, and in His resurrection body—and then he saw Him in His glorified body and it knocked him out. It might knock out Sunday morning church-goers to have such a glimpse of Him in His glory. I guarantee you that we would not come out of church the way we generally do. "As He *is*." Jesus Christ is the Eternal Contemporary. All the false messiahs of this world are dead and buried. Mohammed, Confucius and Buddha are dead. We do not visit the mausoleum of a dead Saviour. There is a sepulcher in Jerusalem which some say is the grave where they buried Him *but He is not in it!*

No mortal can with Him compare
Among the sons of men.

The infinitude of Jesus Christ never leaves Him in a past tense. He forever *is!*

The text goes on to say: "As he is, *so are we!*" Christians are like Him in kind, but not in degree. If we have truly trusted Him we are partakers of His nature and what is His is ours. The text does not say "As he is so we should be" or "shall be." In a Christian, Christ lives again. If you say, "But I don't see many professing Christians who bear much resemblance to Him," I answer that most of them may be just church members or babes in the faith who need to grow by spiritual food, rest and exercise until Christ is formed in them. Christians are the salt of the earth and the light of the world. If only we would be what we are!

And finally the text says, "As he is, so are we *in this world.*" "Like Him" of all things! And "in this world" of all places! Not just in church on Sunday where it is not too difficult to look pious, or in some favored spot "far from the maddening crowd's ignoble strife," but in this foul, wicked world, this perverted Sodom and Gomorrah, in the old rat race every day. Jesus lived in this world and had nowhere to lay His head. He had a hard time here and left us a legacy of tribulation and suffering, and we must take our share of what is left in the fellowship of that suffering. This world is not our home. It is no friend of grace "to help us on to God." It is no more kindly disposed toward Jesus Christ than it ever was. He said it hated Him and would hate us. I hope we remember that when we sing at church so casually, "To the old rugged cross I will ever be true, its shame and reproach gladly bear." If you are under any illusions about the attitude of this world toward Jesus Christ, try really living for Him for a week and you will soon find out!

He said, "As thou (the Father) hast sent me into the world, even so have I also sent them into the world." What we *believe* is important, but a man may believe correctly with his head and still be without any change of heart. What we *do* is important, but a man may do what a Christian ought to do and still be an unconverted Pharisee. Creed and conduct have their place but we are dealing here with character; not what we believe and do, but what we *are*. "So *are* we in this world." A man is not the sum total of what he thinks in his head and does with his hands, but what he is in his heart. Christians are not just nice people. They are new creatures. If you are what you have always been you are not a Christian. A Christian is something new; old things have passed away and all things are become new.

The Scriptures tell us that Christians are married to Christ. When a woman marries a man she takes him for all he is, for better or worse—and sometimes he turns out to be worse than she took him for! When we receive Christ as Saviour and Lord, all that He has becomes ours and all we have becomes His. It is high time we discovered the magnitude of this exchange when we equate it with just joining a church.

All things are His and all things are ours, except ourselves. We are not our own; "we are bought with a price." We are Christ's and Christ is God's. His friends are our friends. "Ye are my friends, if ye do whatsoever I command you." A friend of Jesus is one who obeys Him. That automatically rules out a multitude of church members! What we call fellowship sometimes when we gossip over our coffee at a church supper is often just sociability under religious auspices and not the communion of saints.

His enemies are our enemies. Paul writes of "enemies of the cross of Christ." The friend of the world is the enemy of God. A wife who is eighty-five percent faithful to her husband is not faithful at all. Christians cannot be popular with a world that crucified the Saviour. As the Master so must the servant be. His cross is ours. Simeon prophesied that Jesus would be "spoken against." The Jews in Rome said of the cause of Christ, "Everywhere it is spoken against"—not popular. We who follow Him must ever consent to be called the scum of the earth, a spectacle to the world for the scandal of the cross.

His future is our future. If we suffer with Him we shall also reign with Him. We shall inherit the earth and judge the world. And in the world to come,

> Then we shall be where we would be,
> Then we shall be what we should be;
> Things that are not now, nor could be,
> Soon shall be our own.

It may not look it now but Satan has only a lease on this earth; we have the deed!

Are you married to the Heavenly Bridegroom? I invite you to the greatest of all altars to say: "I take Jesus. His life shall be my life, His joys my joys, His sorrows my sorrows, His friends my friends, His cross my cross, not just until death but for time and eternity, I am His and He is mine.

> O Jesus, I have promised to serve Thee to the end.
> Be Thou forever near me, my Master and my friend.
> I shall not fear the battle if Thou art by my side,
> Nor wander from the pathway if Thou wilt be my Guide."

For *as He is, so are we in this world!*

40

"Sweeter as the Years Go By"

It happened many years ago; I do not remember where. But I will never forget it. I started to the Sunday evening service. Across on a distant hill a black congregation was singing as only our black friends can sing:

> Sweeter as the years go by,
> Sweeter as the years go by;
> Jesus' love is sweeter, richer, fuller, deeper;
> Sweeter as the years go by.

I have never forgotten the blessing of that moment. I am sure the singers meant it. No doubt the lives of many of them were full of drudgery and toil. They knew sorrow and heartache and the satisfactions of life were few; luxuries were nonexistent. But they could still sing, "Nobody knows de trouble I've seen" and end with "Glory, hallelujah!" And they had found that the love of God grew sweeter as the years went by. They could sing, "Sometimes I feel like a motherless child" while trusting a Father who cared. And they could "steal away to Jesus" as they reflected, "I ain't got long to stay here."

To those who sneer that the Christian faith is a delusion, I can only say with pity, "My friend, we poor mortals may be dumb and stupid but we're not that stupid." Don't tell me that for two thousand years God's people have rested their weary heads and soothed their aching hearts and calmed their tormenting fears with a hallucination. The resurrection hope would have been relegated to limbo long since. The best apologists for the faith are not scholars in seclusion pondering heavy tomes and working out theological equations. Ask the millions who have given the love of God a try for fifty years maybe and can say now with more assurance than ever, to use the imagery of a great Gospel song:

> Could we with ink the ocean fill,
> And were the skies of parchment made,
> Were every stalk on earth a quill,
> And every man a scribe by trade,
> To write the love of God above,
> Would drain the ocean dry.
> Nor could the scroll contain the whole,
> Though stretched from sky to sky.

There are times in the mad rush of today's "delirium tremens" that I want to stop for a moment and just listen if perchance, borne on the wings of memory, there may drift back across the years the consolation of that song I heard one Sunday at eventide. I do not need weighty arguments from learned scribes half so much as to be aware afresh that

> Jesus loves me, this I know,
> For the Bible tells me so.

Let me hear rather from God's pilgrims headed for a city with foundations, who have traveled long on the Straight and Narrow Way and have learned that they do not walk alone. They are "the proof of this pudding." Men and women judged ordinary by earthly standards, who never made newspaper headlines, have proved what skeptics have spent a lifetime trying to unravel. While infidels shriek their defiance and wicked men shout their hatred of God, it is all refuted by a few real Christians simply affirming that

> Jesus' love is sweeter, richer, fuller, deeper;
> Sweeter as the years go by.

41

Synthetics

It is a great day for country music. Some of it is authentic but we bemoan the phonies. The drugstore cowboy has been around for years but now there are hillbillies from Long Island and mountaineers from Milwaukee and Appalachians from Amarillo and Blue Ridge banjoists from the Bronx. They never saw Grandfather Mountain or Maggie Valley and when they try, "Let me sleep in your barn tonight, Mister" we want to weep.

If you ain't been there you can't fake it. I grew up in the hills and "Red River Valley" is not a foreign language to me. These modern hicks can't help it but they don't know how. They never grew up on a red dirt farm, never went coon hunting or to corn shuckings and camp meetings or to a one-teacher country school. They never took off on a cold winter morning down a dirt road with a piece of fatback and a cold sweet potato for lunch; never drank water with all the other kids from the same bucket and the same dipper. They never started the day with molasses and pork gravy and closed it with a supper of cornbread and milk.

It is a day of synthetics and it has invaded even the Church. Counterfeit Christian experience can be made to appear so real as to puzzle the very elect. Artificial flowers can seem so genuine as to look better than the real, and hothouse varieties can show up more favorably than lilies of the field exposed to wind and rain. Our Lord told us that preachers who have prophesied, done mighty works and cast out demons will be condemned at the Judgment as workers of iniquity. Christian joy can be imitated and the work of the spirit simulated. The sin against the Holy Spirit lies in ascribing the work of God to the devil. Today we see the work of the devil attributed to God.

Long ago Lorenzo of Florence put on a pageant of Pentecost. He had the twelve apostles lined up down front and at a given time real fire was to fall. But something went wrong. The fire fell but the apostles were set aflame, the curtains ignited, the building caught on fire and the people barely escaped with their lives. Something like that always happens when we try to stage a synthetic Pentecost!

No city product can really capture the spirit of the hills. Only those who are colonists of heaven can sing the language of Zion. Others sing the Lord's song in a strange land like the captives in Babylon. Standing "on Jordan's stormy banks" casting "a wishful eye, to Canaan's fair and happy land, where our possessions lie," is not to be confused with dwelling in Beulah Land. You have to be a citizen of the Kingdom to sing the songs of the King.

Jesus called play-actors, hypocrites, those who act out a synthetic faith. One gets from these phonies the same impression that comes with listening to a cowpoke from Brooklyn trying to sing realistically "When It's Springtime in the Rockies."

A Christian is an exile and alien in this world. He is a citizen of heaven making his way through this earth. He was born into that country; he did not take out naturalization papers. His heart dwells in that land even while his feet tread the dirt down here. He is a pilgrim and a stranger, his home is not here but yonder, he has no certain dwelling place in these lowlands. Anyone else is as out of pitch and place singing spiritual songs as a boy from the metropolis trying to sing a ballad of the mountains.

42

Just a Word

This is an age of unprecedented wastefulness. We are prodigal in our utter misuse of time, energy, ability, our bodies, minds and souls. We squander the treasures of time and talent, burning the candle at both ends, a generation of spendthrifts.

In no other area do we throw away more valuables than in the world of words. Words are so plentiful, they are cheap and common, the supply is unlimited; we take them for granted. The printing presses grind them out by the billion, the air waves are loaded with language, and we never give a thought to this coinage we spent so recklessly and carelessly without a moment's thought as to whose image and superscription they bear. Yet words are the vehicle of thought and far from being so plentiful as to be cheap, they are of infinite value. One word can pack more power than a nuclear bomb. Indeed one word by a crazed fanatic could push a button that would destroy half a world. One "yes" from somebody's sweetheart could mean a wife and the joy of true love or it could mean a surrender to sin and shame. "No" could mean the end of a career, the fading of a dream, the closing of a door to what might have been a great life. There is no way on earth to measure the hidden potential of one little word. If you read one travel sign the wrong way you may miss your destination. No wonder we are told, "let your yea be yea, and your nay, nay." Playing with words is a dangerous game.

And how careless we are in the choice of these words! Sometimes there are a dozen different words that will express something of the thought we want to get across. But in our hurry we grab the first one that comes to mind and it does not convey at all the idea we mean to voice. A jewel of thought may be boxed in a sorry container and the receiver of the gift may rate the diamond by the way we wrapped it.

Consider the word we should have said and didn't. The agony of regret over the kind and loving things we could have uttered but never found time and now the ears that never heard them are closed forever. Or the awful thing we did say and have spent hours upon hours bemoaning and would give all we possess to cancel from the past. "A word fitly spoken is like apples of gold in pictures of silver," but some of us have accumulated bushels of apples of another variety!

"God is in heaven, and thou upon earth: therefore let thy words be few." An attitude of worship can cut down an avalanche of words. And never forget that words shape destiny. "Every idle word that men shall speak, they shall give account thereof in the day of judgment. For by thy words thou shalt be justified, and by thy words thou shalt be condemned." If that ever got through to this generation there would be a mighty wave of "No comment!"

When the great ocean liner, the *Titanic,* went down in 1912 two lists were posted in the ship's home offices. One list was marked "Lost" the other "Saved." What a difference one word made in the eyes of the anxious beholders! Humanity falls ultimately into only two lists in the sight of God. He that believes is not condemned, but he that believes not is condemned already. It is high time we made certain about where we stand as to "Lost" or "Saved." It is just a word's difference but it makes a world's distance—and an eternity's difference!

43

"Awhile"

I love the well-known cowboy ballad, "Red River Valley." It is the haunting plea of a lone rider of the range for his departing sweetheart:

> Come and sit by my side if you love me,
> Do not hasten to bid me adieu,
> But remember the Red River Valley,
> And the cowboy who loved you so true.

He goes on to lament her soon departure:

> From this valley they say you are going,
> We will miss your bright eyes and sweet smile,
> For they say you are taking the sunshine,
> That brightens our pathway awhile.

One day I found myself humming my own edition of this love song in honor of my sweetheart who walked life's way with me for over thirty years:

> Come and sit by my side if you hear me;
> Do not hasten to bid me adieu.
> For I'm walking a long, lonesome valley,
> This traveler who loved you so true.

> Days are long since you left me for heaven.
> How I've missed your bright eyes and sweet smile!
> For you took all the joy and the sunshine
> That brightened my pathway awhile.

I'll soon catch up with you where you're waiting,
I've not lost you, I know where you are;
As the days swiftly pass I will find you,
I don't think you can be very far.

She certainly brightened my pathway *awhile.* I leaf through diaries of our travels all over America. Memory recaptures waiting in train stations, riding across the desert, sunrise and sunset, happy gatherings and precious friends, gracious dinners in countless homes, the anticipation of meeting again after separations, that daily letter in the motel box. It covered a long span but now it seems only "awhile." It is the lonely day and night that stretches endlessly.

Many bereaved friends of mine have remarried in a hurry. That is their business and I am glad they have found a new companion. But I like my line, "Do not hasten to bid me adieu." I cannot part quickly with the other half of my life. But awhile is not forever. I do not understand the heavenly arrangement and I know there will be differences; but they will be improvements. "Somehow, somewhere, meet we must" and the heavenly will not be a pale copy but a glorious fulfillment.

Awhile is exactly what it claims to be; it is a while. Some of life's whiles are dark and agonizing. Some seem endless in their sheer loneliness and dreariness. Some are so joyous that hours seem but minutes. Our happy whiles here are but a foretaste of forevers to come. God will not smash to pieces at death the vessels that held so much delight. "What is holiest here below must forever live and grow." What brightened our pathway here awhile will resume under better conditions forever.

44

Excursion Into Yesterday

Solitary strolls are as much a part of my life as meat and potatoes but this ramble was something special. It was part of a visit to my boyhood home in the hills. It was a Sunday morning in May and I had not been "home" in the springtime for many, many years. I wondered if I might recapture some of the ecstasy I had known over half a century ago. I broke away from the home folks as one who had an important and pressing engagement to fill. I did indeed have a date with a boyhood long departed.

From a closet I recovered an old walking stick notched and carved and inscribed with a date back in 1927. It had been my companion on many a jaunt and carrying it now restored at the very start a rapport with gentler days and sweeter times before life took on the tempo of the last mad decades.

I started down an old pasture trail in the mood of whoever wrote that dear nostalgic gem:

> I wandered today to the hill, Maggie
> To watch the scene below,
> The creek and the creaking old mill, Maggie,
> As we used to do long ago.

With every step I laid aside some of the accumulated burden of the years and my pace quickened until I was astonished at how I fairly skipped along at a gait that belied my approaching threescore years and ten. I soon found myself back in a world I had lost. Down deep in the hollow the din of traffic, the roar of jets, the pandemonium of "Progress"(!) was shut out and

111

everything was just as it used to be. For the great elemental things do not change; they do not try to get in step with man's deliriums. The bobwhite sounded like the bobwhites of my boyhood. The indigo bunting had not added any new notes and the little prairie warbler ran his octave trill with the same perfection his remote ancestors had mastered long before. The yellow-breasted chat, that clown of the bird world, was up to the old tricks—the ventriloquism, the odd gestures, the ludicrous antics, the melodramatics—just like his forbears in my early days when I used to wonder what feathered lunatic had invaded the premises. The little field sparrow was in full swing and from the woods nearby the wood thrush sang as sweetly as when long ago in the early morning or at "milking time" other wood thrushes closed the day with their vespers.

It was all just like it used to be and for one precious hour I closed the door on an insane age and withdrew into a chapel far from the maddening crowds' ignoble strife. I could not stay for I had to return to what somehow has got itself called an advanced stage of civilization. But for a blessed interval I turned off the switch and cut off the connection and was a country boy again. If enough of us could make such escapes, find time and place to cool our fevered spirits and renew our faith, there might still be hope for this demented generation. Our Lord set us the example long ago and He holds the answer to all our futile strivings if men would trust Him and walk with Him the path of peace.

I was amazed at the alacrity with which I climbed the hill back up to the top of the ridge just as I did fifty years ago when I hoed corn down at the creek. It is a miracle what one short hour can do to revive the drooping spirits of a tired preacher on an all-too-brief excursion into yesterday.

45

Lonesome Valley

I was invited some time ago to speak to a Single Adults Conference in a Texas church. They asked me to speak at least once on the subject of loneliness. It seemed to be one of their greatest problems. It is a major problem with millions today. America has the highest per capita rate of boredom of any nation on earth. Yet no other people on earth are entertained as much as Americans. The amusement business is a top activity today. It goes on day and night by radio and television. It packs theatres, stadiums, even churches (Lord, help us!). Loneliness fills psychiatrists' offices and mental hospitals, and drives to drink and drugs, insanity and suicide. It is as bad in a crowd as in solitude. Americans travel all over the world trying to get away from it but it sticks closer than a brother. It can bring a curse or a blessing. If you master it, it pays rich dividends. If it masters you, woe unto you!

When my Texas friends asked me to talk about loneliness, I felt that I could qualify. I have graduated and taken postgraduate courses. For nearly forty years I was a bachelor preacher with no certain dwelling place. Then the loneliness was broken for thirty-three years by a precious companion. But she went home to heaven and I entered Lonesome Valley again. I wrote *Though I Walk Through The Valley* and began to preach more to troubled and lonely hearts. The rewards have been beyond words to relate. I have become a comforter of the bereaved and brokenhearted. You have to walk that valley to know what it is like. Mere philosophizing, even with the best of intentions, won't do it. The sorrowing know the difference and turn away.

I heard of a dear soul who listened during a meeting to the spiritual, "Balm In Gilead." She thought they said "Bomb In Gilead" and moaned, "My soul, bombs are going off everywhere else and now they're bombing Gilead!" It does look like it sometimes everywhere. It is a shell-shocked generation. It is Bomb or Balm! But there is a balm for our healing.

As the old spiritual puts it, we must walk this Lonesome Valley. We must walk it for ourselves. Nobody else can walk it for us. We must walk it for ourselves. But loneliness has its rewards. We are a gregarious generation today and cannot endure our own company so we fall on all sorts of devices to avoid solitude. Radio and television blare all day and most of the night. They are the first things on in the morning and last off at bedtime. No greater calamity can be imagined by the average American than a rainy day without television. Preachers, of all people, should have the most time to be quiet but a preacher strolling along just thinking would be eyed with suspicion by church members who wonder why he isn't at the committee meeting of the Sons and Daughters of I Will Arise.

When that Lonesome Valley becomes a Must for some reason or other we begin to discover how paltry our inner resources are. Look out for it and store up spiritual food in advance. Lonesome Valley is bad enough any time but it is disaster when you enter with an undernourished soul.

46

"Until"

I sit this morning on the Mount of Olives overlooking Jerusalem. It is very early and the old city glows in the light of the rising sun. I see not a soul stirring anywhere. Somewhere on this Mount my Lord gave the great Olivet Discourse about the fall of Jerusalem and the end of the age. Somewhere here He wept over the city. Down below I see the traditional Garden of Gethsemane. Somewhere from this Mount the Saviour ascended into heaven. Somewhere on this Mount He will come again.

Before me lies the greatest city of all time, greatest in its past and future and greatest now because of what it was and will be. Here is the center of earth and everything flows toward it even as the languages to the west of it read from left to right and the languages to the east read from right to left. Here is the key to history for if a man does not understand the meaning of Jerusalem past and future the rest of history is a hopeless puzzle.

Jesus loved this Mount of Olives. I have just come from the Sea of Galilee, the other favored spot He visited so often. In both places He found solitude and respite from the pressures of both the friendly multitude and bitter enemies. We read that after one conference of officers, chief priests and Pharisees, "Every man went unto his own house. Jesus went unto the Mount of Olives." So today His enemies go their own way and plot their own schemes but if you want to find Him in today's picture, sit on the Mount of Olives and read His words. Jerusalem knew not the time of her visitation and still does not know. He would have gathered her children as a hen gathers her chickens but they would not. She persecuted the prophets and had such a reputation for it that the Saviour said it was unthinkable that a prophet should perish outside Jerusalem. But He is not through with that city for He said, "Ye shall not see me henceforth till ye shall say, Blessed is he that cometh in the name of the Lord."

This morning I thrill with delight that I am on the Mount where my Lord will stand when He returns. Toward this divine event the whole creation moves. Let politicians and potentates meet in marble halls and wrestle with the problems of this bewildered old world, never so vexed as today; but here is where the answer will be revealed. East and West meet here. Three great religions center here. This old city glows with an importance not her own. She glows because she is the city of David and David's Son who is scheduled by the timetables of God to sit on David's throne.

Israel today looks for Messiah to come the first time. Christians are looking for Him to come the second time. "Until the fulness of the Gentiles be come in"; "Until the times of the Gentiles be fulfilled"; "Until they shall say, Blessed is he that cometh in the name of the Lord." I am living in The Great Until. What time is it? It is *until.* Recently a dear Christian brother closed his letter to me not with "Yours truly" but "Until"!

So this morning this country preacher as he sits on the Mount of Olives surveying Jerusalem is not waiting for something to happen; he is waiting for Someone to come. He is not looking for signs; he is listening for a sound, the voice of the archangel and the trumpet of God. A while ago millions watched a man set foot on the moon. Would that this poor distracted world looked as intently for the Messiah to set foot on this mountain!

47

Mid-Summer Lament

It is the middle of July and a heat wave. Soon the wood thrush will end his flute program for this year. I cross the street each day into the college woods to listen to my favorite singer. He turns time backward in its flight and makes me a boy again back on the little farm listening to the early morning and late afternoon programs of this beloved artist. He reminds me of the Bible word about creation groaning and travailing in pain awaiting the manifestation of the sons of God. In his songs I catch the plaintive undertones of a wistful longing for a redeemed earth.

The red, red robin is still "bob, bob, bobbin' along" but although many of them winter in the north, to me he always is the harbinger of spring and I shall miss him through snow and ice until his "cheerily, cheer-up" tells me happy days are here again. The meadowlark and song sparrow greet me along my favorite path early in the morning. Of course some of my feathered songsters stay here all winter but the music will soon die down and we shall sigh, "The melancholy days have come, the saddest of the year." I usually go to one of my conference grounds in time to hear the hooded warbler who makes his headquarters each year along my trail. I am loath to see the summer pass and would trade it in for spring anytime . . . and night for day.

Nature has many faces and the lovely scenes in the nature magazines do not tell all the story. Spring blossoms and autumn colors are offset by scenes of flood and tornado. Recently in New Jersey I watched an adorable flock of twelve tiny baby

117

ducks take to the water every morning. Twelve little balls of
yellow down captured my heart. But two mornings later I noticed that there were now only nine of them. "Turtles got three
of them yesterday," I was told. I wanted to declare vengeance
on all turtles but remembered that turtles are part of God's
creation and they must make their way as their custom is, even
nibbling dainty morsels like baby ducks. I do remember, however, that the Scriptures predict an end to the law of tooth and
claw one day, with the lion and the lamb lying down together—and the lamb not inside the lion! The evolutionists will
scoff at such a final chapter but some of us believe in the re-
demption of creation from the curse of sin. Creation groans, we
groan, the Holy Spirit groans for us in prayer. We believe
groans will give way to glory!

It must be clear to the dullest that something evidently went
wrong with the original creation. It was not the intention of our
God to begin with a world of beauty mixed with horror, millions slaughtered by weather gone wild. It started with a Garden and it will be consummated in a Paradise. So I put up with
floods and tornadoes, sickness and death, all the weird disasters that make no sense now.

I am told of a day to come when all these weird and woeful
happenings will be forever past. A little boy was puzzled by an
old song and asked, "Dad, what do they mean by singing
about that place called *Dynamore?*" He knew there was a Bal-
timore but this was a city not on his map. Well, we are going
home to *"Die no more"* and that City is on God's map!

The hush of summer music as autumn nears reminds me
that even winter passes and spring has always made it. If He
comes before spring, we will change calendars for eternity
where they count not time by years. For the Christian, *that* is
worth waiting for a spell, whatever that spell may bring!

48

Church in the Wildwood

This week I preached for four days in a country church in a picture-card setting that brings back memories of a quieter and sweeter past. Each evening before the service I walked out on a road by the beautifully kept cemetery and looked back on the rural meeting house among the trees. The wood thrush was singing in the woods behind me. Nearby is a highway but it is not a main artery and traffic was light. I felt that I had escaped for a few hours the "delirium tremens" of progress and had reverted to something approaching sanity.

I told the young pastor that he had better think hard and pray much before he allowed himself to leave this haven for the frantic turmoil of a town or city charge. Once I had such a pastorate and when I resigned I prepared an article describing what I was giving up. When I read the article I almost withdrew my resignation!

This is not mere sentiment nor nostalgia for the good old days. This generation has painted itself into a corner and created a technological monster that now feeds on its creators. Human minds and bodies cannot stand the pressures and unless we can create a modern equivalent to the life we once had time to live, we are going to be smothered under the debris of a civilization that collapsed in the wreckage of its own culture.

Our religious life had better get back to the church in the wildwood and learn a few things. For too long we have tried to get in step with this age. Christian periodicals are top-heavy with wordy dissertations utterly beyond the comprehension of the man on the street. New theology and philosophy may please the literati up in the intellectual stratosphere but the average working man cannot buy encyclopedias and lexicons to unravel all this highbrow verbiage. At the other extreme we have gone all-out on sex and the new woman and subjective experiences to tickle the curiosity of Athenians always listening for some new thing. It has not dawned upon most of us that we do not need some new thing so much as some old things that would be new if anybody tried them! We had better get out of the novelty shop and return to the antique shop!

It has been a refreshing four days with the church in the wildwood. The meetings convinced me anew that people are hungry for the old message preached in simple terms. Our Lord set the example with His parables taken from the common things of everyday life.

I have had my threescore and ten, with a ten-year bonus, and more doors are open than ever before with a backlog of invitations I cannot accept. I have no promotion gimmicks, not even brochures with my picture (if I tried that, all doors would close!). This simply demonstrates to me that if one will speak as God bids him he will not lack for an opportunity. Millions of weary hearts thirst for the plain living water. I heard recently of a taster in a bottling plant who was moving along blind-folded, testing new fancy concoctions. A glass of plain drinking water had been put at the end of the row to be tested. The taster moved along smacking his lips. When he tried the water he observed, "I don't know what this is but it won't sell!" Well, plain water may not sell but people drink it more than all the pop and colas.

I think I'll stick to the plain Living Water, for no substitute has ever come along that works.

49

Candidate for Promotion

Kipling had it right when he wrote,

> We shall rest, and, faith, we shall need it,
>   —lie down for an aeon or two,
> Till the Master of All Good Workmen
>   shall put us to work anew.

The average Christian is in pitiful ignorance as to what we do in the life to come. Heaven is not an endless vacation where we sit on clouds wearing haloes and plucking harps forever. Nothing could be more exhausting than eternally doing nothing. Indeed the Scriptures indicate more vocation than vacation. "His servants shall serve Him" in the New Jerusalem. The Master will make the faithful servant ruler over all He has. We shall have authority over five cities, over ten cities. If we suffer with Him we shall reign with Him. The saints shall judge the world. We shall sit on twelve thrones, judging the twelve tribes of Israel. Our jurisdiction may extend to other worlds and we shall never grow tired in whatever we are doing.

One thing is certain; we are being prepared for it now. And our promotion there will be governed by our record here.

> Take time to be holy, be calm in thy soul—
> Each thought and each motive beneath His control.
> Thus led by His Spirit to fountains of love,
> Thou soon shalt be fitted *for service above.*

This world is not our boot camp, this is the war! We are in the battle now! But we are training for our service in heaven after the war is over. And why should we not seek a reward? "So run that ye may obtain." Paul looked for a crown and a prize. It is not the main motivation, for our business is to glorify God. But we do need some sanctified ambition among the saints today, ambition to possess the best that God has for us. Whatever we do in the ages to come, think how important are these few years on earth for all eternity hereafter! When I see the nonchalant crowd in church on Sunday morning and note how casually they take being Christians, I fear that we have misread our script and have not begun to realize what it means to be children of God getting ready to reign over a redeemed earth through an endless eternity. The Scriptures indicate degrees of Reward in the world to come. I cannot believe that one who built a cheap life with wood, hay and stubble—that will go up in smoke when "the day shall declare it"—will be equally rewarded with the saint who has been an architect in gold, silver and precious stones.

If we are to reign one day as kings, should we not live like princes now? Sometimes the training may mean a furnace of affliction, sorrow, heartache, a thorn in the flesh. God wants special saints with postgraduate degrees for high positions in the world to come.

Are you a candidate for promotion? What is the basis for that promotion? "Thou hast been faithful over a few things, I will make thee ruler over many things." Not flashy, fitful, famous (and certainly not fantastic or fabulous)—just faithful. It is required of stewards that a man be found faithful. Anybody can be faithful but not many are. Paul was faithful to the faith, to the fight and to the finish. The greatest ability is dependability. We read that Gaius did *faithfully* whatever he did. He was in line for promotion!

50

Nearer Home

It has been a long day in the little Florida town where I'm staying and preaching this week. Living for forty years in motels, week by week readjusting to a new bed, food, climate and circumstances in general, is no picnic. Billy Graham said recently that he felt the weight of thirty years of hotel life. What will he say after he is eighty years of age!

Next week I hope to return for a few days to my apartment. Of course there will be no one at the door to greet me and I may swallow hard when I set my bags down inside. It has been that way for over eight years now and I never get used to it; I just live with it as do many others.

Yesterday there came to mind those precious lines by Phoebe Cary:

> One sweetly solemn thought
> Comes to me o'er and o'er;
> I am nearer home today
> Than I ever have been before.

All day I've been saying it, "One day nearer home!" I sat alone in the dining room at supper and looked at other guests, some drinking their cocktails. I felt no superiority for, left to myself, I am no better than they. Whatever difference there may be is only because of the grace of God. I'm only a pilgrim headed home, a stranger with no dwelling place down here. Sara used to sing, "This world is not my home, I'm only passing through." She has arrived and now I follow. People sometimes ask, "Would you like to live your life over again?" I reply,

"No, I'm too near home!" The loneliness of midnight, waking in strange places, staring at blank walls, subconsciously looking still for her letters that never come, the irresistible desire to whisper in the darkness, "Honey, are you awake?"—like I used to do—all is bearable because I'm not lengthening the distance between us; I'm shortening it as I draw nearer to where she is now!

I have thought and read much about our heavenly home. I am sure the magnificence of the City will be a grandeur that would overwhelm us in our present state of body and mind. Yet I note that our Lord said it so simply: "In my Father's house are many dwelling places. I go to prepare a place for you. I will return to get you to live in my home forever." There is an at-homeness about that that does not dazzle us; instead, we'll feel "at home." We'll not be strangers over there and I have a feeling that with all the glory of the Heavenly City there will be an everlasting relaxation in the Land of No More—no more sin, sorrow, death, sickness, pain.

When Augustine's mother wanted to accompany him on a trip he thought she had better not try it at her age. She might die. She replied, "My life is hid with Christ in God. If God is my home, how can I die away from home!"

Making yourself at home in God now is a good "getting-ready" for heaven. When we arrive at the house made ready in the heavens, it will be glorious beyond our poor words to say. But we'll feel at home. For that is where we'll be!